A Treatise on the Gift of Perseverance

A Treatise on the Gift of Perseverance

St. Augustine

A Treatise on the Gift of Perseverance

© Lighthouse Publishing 2018

Written by: St. Augustine (Nov.13 354 – Aug.28 430)
Translated by Peter Holmes and Robert Ernest Wallis
Revised by: Professor Benjamin B. Warfield, D.D
Updated into Modern U.S English by A.M. Overett (b. 1960)

All rights reserved. Without limiting the rights under copyright reserved above, no part of this publication may be reproduced, stored in a retrieval system, or transmitted, in any form or by any means (electronic, mechanical, photocopying, recording or otherwise), without the prior written permission of the copyright owner of this book.

Published by
Lighthouse Christian Publishing
SAN 257-4330
5531 Dufferin Drive
Savage, Minnesota, 55378
United States of America

www.lighthousechristianpublishing.com

A TREATISE ON THE GIFT OF PERSEVERANCE

BY AURELIUS AUGUSTIN, BISHOP OF HIPPO;

Being the Second Book,

Of the Treatise "On the Predestination of the Saints."

addressed to prosper and Hilary. A.D. 428 or 429

In the first part of the book he proves that the perseverance by which a man perseveres in Christ to the end is God's gift; for that it is a mockery to ask of God that which is not believed to be given by God. Moreover, that in the Lord's prayer scarcely anything is asked for but perseverance, according to the exposition of the martyr Cyprian, by which exposition the enemies to this grace were convicted before they were born. He teaches that the grace of perseverance is not given according to the merits of the receivers, but to some it is given by God's mercy; to others it is not given, by His righteous judgment. That it is inscrutable why, of adults, one rather than another should be called; just as, moreover, of two infants it is inscrutable why the one should be taken, the other left. But that it is still more inscrutable why, of two pious persons, to one it should be given to persevere, to the other it should not be given; but that this is most certain, that the former is of the predestinated, the latter is not. He observes that the mystery of predestination is set forth in our Lord's words concerning the people of Tyre and Sidon, who would have repented if the same miracles had been done among them which had been done in Chorazin. He shows that the case of infants is of force to confirm the truth of predestination and grace in older people; and he answers the passage of his third book on free will, unsoundly alleged on this point by his adversaries. Subsequently, in the second part of this work, he rebuts what they say, —to wit, that the definition of predestination is opposed to the usefulness of exhortation and rebuke. He asserts, on the other hand, that it is advantageous to preach predestination, so that man may not glory in himself, but in the Lord. As to the objections, however, which they make against predestination, he shows that the same objections may be twisted in no unlike manner either against God's foreknowledge or against that grace which they all agree to be necessary for other good things (except for the beginning of faith and the completion of perseverance). For that the predestination of the saints is nothing else than God's foreknowledge and preparation for His benefits, by which whoever are delivered are most certainly delivered. But he bids that predestination should be preached in a harmonious manner, and not in such a way as to seem to an unskillful multitude as if it were disproved by its very preaching. Lastly, he commends to us Jesus Christ, as placed before our eyes, as the most eminent instance of predestination.

Chapter 1 [I.]—Of the Nature of the Perseverance Here Discoursed of.

I Have now to consider the subject of perseverance with greater care; for in the former book also I said some things on this subject when I was discussing the beginning of faith. I assert, therefore, that the perseverance by which we persevere in Christ even to the end is the gift of God; and I call that the end by which is finished that life wherein alone there is peril of falling. Therefore, it is uncertain whether any one has received this gift so long as he is still alive. For if he fall before he dies, he is, of course, said not to have persevered; and most truly is it said. How, then, should he be said to have received or to have had perseverance who has not persevered? For if anyone have continence, and fall away from that virtue and become incontinent,—or, in like manner, if he have righteousness, if patience, if even faith, and fall away, he is rightly said to have had these virtues and to have them no longer; for he was continent, or he was righteous, or he was patient, or he was believing, as long as he was so; but when he ceased to be so, he no longer is what he was. But how should he who has not persevered have ever been persevering, since it is only by persevering that any one shows himself persevering, —and this he has not done? But lest anyone should object to this, and say, If from the time at which any one became a believer he has lived—for the sake of argument—ten years, and in the midst of them has fallen from the faith, has he not persevered for five years? I am not contending about words. If it be thought that this also should be called perseverance, as it were for so long as it lasts, assuredly he is not to be said to have had in any degree that perseverance of which we are now discoursing, by which one perseveres in Christ even to the end. And the believer of one year, or of a period as much shorter as may be conceived of, if he has lived faithfully until he died, has rather had this perseverance than the believer of many years' standing, if a little time before his death he has fallen away from the steadfastness of his faith.

Chapter 2 [II.]—Faith is the Beginning of a Christian Man. Martyrdom for Christ's Sake is His Best Ending.

This matter being settled, let us see whether this perseverance, of which it was said, "He that persevere unto the end, the same shall be saved," is a gift of God. And if it be not, how is that saying of the apostle true: "Unto you it is given in the behalf of Christ, not only to believe on Him, but also to suffer for His sake"? Of these things, certainly, one has respect to the beginning, the other to the end. Yet each is the gift of God, because both are said to be given; as, also, I have already said above. For what is more truly the beginning for a Christian than to believe in Christ? What end is better than to suffer for Christ? But so far as pertains to believing in Christ, whatever kind of contradiction has been discovered, that not the beginning but the increase of faith should be called God's gift, —to this opinion, by God's gift, I have answered enough, and more than enough. But what reason can be given why perseverance to the end should not be given in Christ to him to whom it is given to suffer for Christ, or, to speak more distinctly, to whom it is given to die for Christ? For the Apostle Peter, showing that this is the gift of God, says, "It is better, if the will of God be so, to suffer for well-doing than for evil-doing." When he says, "If the will of God be so," he shows that this is divinely given, and yet not to all saints, to suffer for Christ's sake. For certainly those whom the will of God does not will to attain to the experience and the glory of suffering, do not fail to attain to the kingdom of God if they persevere in Christ to the end. But who can say that this perseverance is not given to those who die in Christ from any weakness of body, or by any kind of accident, although a far more difficult perseverance is given to those by whom even death itself is undergone for Christ's sake? Because perseverance is much more difficult when the persecutor is engaged in preventing a man's perseverance; and therefore, he is sustained in his perseverance unto death. Hence it is more difficult to have the former perseverance, —easier to have the latter; but to Him to whom nothing is difficult it is easy to give both. For God has promised this, saying, "I will put my fear in their hearts, that they may not depart from me." And what else is this than, "Such and so great shall be my fear that I will put into their hearts that they will perseveringly cleave to me"?

Chapter 3. —God is Besought for It, Because It is His Gift.

But why is that perseverance asked for from God if it is not given by God? Is that, too, a mocking petition, when that is asked from Him which it is known that He does not give, but, though He gives it not, is in man's power; just as that giving of thanks is a mockery, if thanks are given to God for that which He did not give nor do?

But what I have said there, I say also here again: "Be not deceived," says the apostle, "God is not mocked." O man, God is a witness not only of your words, but also of your thoughts. If you ask anything in truth and faith of one who is so rich, believe that you receive from Him from whom you ask, what you ask. Abstain from honoring Him with your lips and extolling yourself over Him in your heart, by believing that you have from yourself what you are pretending to beseech from Him. Is not this perseverance, perchance, asked for from Him? He who says this is not to be rebuked by any arguments but must be overwhelmed with the prayers of the saints. Is there any of these who does not ask for himself from God that he may persevere in Him, when in that very prayer which is called the Lord's—because the Lord taught it—when it is prayed by the saints, scarcely anything else is understood to be prayed for but perseverance?

Chapter 4. —Three Leading Points of the Pelagian Doctrine.

Read with a little more attention its exposition in the treatise of the blessed martyr Cyprian, which he wrote concerning this matter, the title of which is, On the Lord's Prayer; and see how many years ago, and what sort of an antidote was prepared against those poisons which the Pelagians were one day to use. For there are three points, as you know, which the catholic Church chiefly maintains against them. One of these is, that the grace of God is not given according to our merits; because even every one of the merits of the righteous is God's gift and is conferred by God's grace. The second is, that no one lives in this corruptible body, however righteous he may be, without sins of some kind. The third is, that man is born obnoxious to the first man's sin, and bound by the chain of condemnation, unless the guilt which is contracted by generation be loosed by regeneration. Of these three points, that which I have placed last is the only one that is not treated of in the above-named book of the glorious martyr; but of the two others the discourse there is of such perspicuity, that the above-named heretics, modern enemies of the grace of Christ, are found to have been convicted long before they were born. Among these merits of the saints, then, which are no merits unless they are the gifts of God, he says that perseverance also is God's gift, in these words: "We say, 'Hallowed be Thy name;' not that we ask for God that He may be hallowed by our prayers, but that we beseech of Him that His name may be hallowed in us. But by whom is God sanctified, since He Himself sanctifies? Well, because He says, Be ye holy because I also am holy, we ask and entreat that we, who were sanctified in baptism, may persevere in that which we have begun to be." And a little after, still arguing about that selfsame matter, and teaching that we entreat perseverance from the Lord, which we could in no wise rightly and truly do unless it were His gift, he says: "We pray that this sanctification may abide in us; and because our Lord and Judge warns the man that was healed and quickened by Him to sin no more, lest a worse thing happen unto him, we make this supplication in our constant prayers; we ask this, day and night, that the sanctification and quickening which is received from the grace of God may be preserved by His protection." That teacher, therefore, understands that we are asking from Him for perseverance in sanctification, that is, that we should persevere in sanctification, when we who are sanctified say, "Hallowed be Thy name." For what else is it to ask for what we have already received, than that it be given to us also not to cease from its possession? As, therefore, the saint, when he asks God that he may be holy, is certainly asking that he may continue to be holy, so certainly the chaste person also, when he asks that he may be chaste, the continent that he may be continent, the righteous that he may be righteous, the pious that he may be pious, and the like,—which things, against the Pelagians, we maintain to be God's gifts,—are asking, without doubt, that they may persevere in those good things which they have acknowledged that they have received. And if they receive this, assuredly they also receive perseverance itself, the great gift of God, whereby His other gifts are preserved.

Chapter 5. —The Second Petition in the Lord's Prayer.

What, when we say, "Thy kingdom come," do we ask else, but that that should also come to us which we do not doubt will come to all saints? And therefore here also, what do they who are already holy pray for, save that they may persevere in that holiness which has been given them? For no otherwise will the kingdom of God come to them; which it is certain will come not to others, but to those who persevere to the end.

Chapter 6 [III.]—The Third Petition. How Heaven and Earth are Understood in the Lord's Prayer.

The third petition is, "Thy will be done in heaven and in earth;" or, as it is read in many codices, and is more frequently made use of by petitioners, "As in heaven, so also in earth," which many people understand, "As the holy angels, so also may we do thy will." That teacher and martyr will have heaven and earth, however, to be understood as spirit and flesh, and says that we pray that we may do the will of God with the full concord of both. He saw in these words also another meaning, congruous to the soundest faith, of which meaning I have already spoken above,—to wit, that for unbelievers, who are as yet earth, bearing in their first birth only the earthly man, believers are understood to pray, who, being clothed with the heavenly man, are not unreasonably called by the name of heaven; where he plainly shows that the beginning of faith also is God's gift, since the holy Church prays not only for believers, that faith may be increased or may continue in them, but, moreover, for unbelievers, that they may begin to have what they have not had at all, and against which, besides, they were indulging hostile feelings. Now, however, I am arguing not concerning the beginning of faith, of which I have already spoken much in the former book, but of that perseverance which must be had even to the end, —which assuredly even the saints, who do the will of God, seek when they say in prayer, "Thy will be done." For, since it is already done in them, why do they still ask that it may be done, except that they may persevere in that which they have begun to be? Nevertheless, it may here be said that the saints do not ask that the will of God may be done in heaven, but that it may be done in earth as in heaven,— that is to say, that earth may imitate heaven, that is, that man may imitate the angel, or that an unbeliever may imitate a believer; and thus that the saints are asking that that may be which is not yet, not that that which is may continue. For, by whatever holiness men may be distinguished, they are not yet equal to the angels of God; not yet, therefore, is the will of God done in them as it is in heaven. And if this be so, in that portion indeed in which we ask that men from unbelievers may become believers, it is not perseverance, but beginning, that seems to be asked for; but in that in which we ask that men may be made equal to the angels of God in doing God's will,—where the saints pray for this, they are found to be praying for perseverance; since no one attains to that highest blessedness which is in the kingdom, unless he shall persevere unto the end in that holiness which he has received on earth.

Chapter 7 [IV.]—The Fourth Petition.

The fourth petition is, "Give us this day our daily bread," where the blessed Cyprian shows how here also perseverance is understood to be asked for. Because he says, among other things, "And we ask that this bread should be given to us daily, that we who are in Christ, and daily receive the Eucharist for the food of salvation, may not by the interposition of some heinous sin be separated from Christ's body by being withheld from communicating and prevented from partaking of the heavenly bread." These words of the holy man of God indicate that the saints ask for perseverance directly from God, when with this intention they say, "Give us this day our daily bread," that they may not be separated from Christ's body, but may continue in that holiness in which they allow no crime by which they may deserve to be separated from it.

Chapter 8 [V.]—The Fifth Petition. It is an Error of the Pelagians that the Righteous are Free from Sin.

In the fifth sentence of the prayer we say, "Forgive us our debts, as we also forgive our debtors," in which petition alone perseverance is not found to be asked for. For the sins which we ask to be forgiven us are past, but perseverance, which saves us for eternity, is indeed necessary for the time of this life; but not for the time which is past, but for that which remains even to its end. Yet it is worth the labor to consider for a little, how even already in this petition the heretics who were to arise long after were transfixed by the tongue of Cyprian, as if by the most invincible dart of truth. For the Pelagians dare to say even this: that the righteous man in this life has no sin at all, and that in such men there is even now a Church not having spot or wrinkle or any such thing, which is the one and only bride of Christ; as if she were not His bride who throughout the whole earth says what she has learnt from Him, "Forgive us our debts." But observe how the most glorious Cyprian destroys these. For when he was expounding that very clause of the Lord's Prayer, he says among other things: "And how necessarily, how providently, and salutary are we admonished that we are sinners, since we are compelled to entreat for our sins; and while pardon is asked for from God, the soul recalls its own consciousness. Lest anyone should flatter himself that he is innocent, and by exalting himself should more deeply perish, he is instructed and taught that he sins daily, in that he is bidden daily to entreat for his sins. Thus, moreover, John also in his Epistle warns us, and says, 'If we say that we have no sin, we deceive ourselves, and the truth is not in us.'" And the rest, which it would be long to insert in this place.

Chapter 9. —When Perseverance is Granted to a Person, He Cannot But Persevere.

Now, moreover, when the saints say, "Lead us not into temptation, but deliver us from evil," what do they pray for but that they may persevere in holiness? For, assuredly, when that gift of God is granted to them, — which is sufficiently plainly shown to be God's gift, since it is asked of Him, —that gift of God, then, being granted to them that they may not be led into temptation, none of the saints fails to keep his perseverance in holiness even to the end. For there is not anyone who ceases to persevere in the Christian purpose unless he is first of all led into temptation. If, therefore, it be granted to him according to his prayer that he may not be led, certainly by the gift of God he persists in that sanctification which by the gift of God he has received.

Chapter 10 [VI.]—The Gift of Perseverance Can Be Obtained by Prayer.

But you write that "these brethren will not have this perseverance so preached as that it cannot be obtained by prayer or lost by obstinacy." In this they are little careful in considering what they say. For we are speaking of that perseverance whereby one perseveres unto the end, and if this is given, one does persevere unto the end; but if one does not persevere unto the end, it is not given, which I have already sufficiently discussed above. Let not men say, then, that perseverance is given to anyone to the end, except when the end itself has come, and he to whom it has been given has been found to have persevered unto the end. Certainly, we say that one whom we have known to be chaste is chaste, whether he should continue or not in the same chastity; and if he should have any other divine endowment which may be kept and lost, we say that he has it as long as he has it; and if he should lose it, we say that he had it. But since no one has perseverance to the end except he who does persevere to the end, many people may have it, but none can lose it. For it is not to be feared that perchance when a man has persevered unto the end, some evil will may arise in him, so that he does not persevere unto the end. This gift of God, therefore, may be obtained by prayer, but when it has been given, it cannot be lost by contumacy. For when any one has persevered unto the end, he neither can lose this gift, nor others which he could lose before the end. How, then, can that be lost, whereby it is brought about that even that which could be lost is not lost?

Chapter 11. —Effect of Prayer for Perseverance.

But, lest perchance it be said that perseverance even to the end is not indeed lost when it has once been given,—that is, when a man has persevered unto the end,—but that it is lost, in some sense, when a man by contumacy so acts that he is not able to attain to it; just as we say that a man who has not persevered unto the end has lost eternal life or the kingdom of God, not because he had already received and actually had it, but because he would have received and had it if he had persevered;—let us lay aside controversies of words, and say that some things even which are not possessed, but are hoped to be possessed, may be lost. Let anyone who dares, tell me whether God cannot give what He has commanded to be asked from Him. Certainly he who affirms this, I say not is a fool, but he is mad. But God commanded that His saints should say to Him in prayer, "Lead us not into temptation." Whoever, therefore, is heard when he asks this, is not led into the temptation of contumacy, whereby he could or would be worthy to lose perseverance in holiness.

Chapter 12. —Of His Own Will a Man Forsakes God, So that He is Deservedly Forsaken of Him.

But, on the other hand, "of his own will a man forsakes God, so as to be deservedly forsaken by God." Who would deny this? But it is for that reason we ask not to be led into temptation, so that this may not happen. And if we are heard, certainly it does not happen, because God does not allow it to happen. For nothing comes to pass except what either He Himself does, or Himself allows to be done. Therefore, He is powerful both to turn wills from evil to good, and to convert those that are inclined to fall, or to direct them into a way pleasing to Himself. For to Him it is not said in vain, "O God, Thou shalt turn again and quicken us;" it is not vainly said, "Give not my foot to be moved;" it is not vainly said, "Give me not over, O Lord, from my desire to the sinner;" finally, not to mention many passages, since probably more may occur to you, it is not vainly said, "Lead us not into temptation." For whoever is not led into temptation, certainly is not led into the temptation of his own evil will; and he who is not led into the temptation of his own evil will, is absolutely led into no temptation. For "everyone is tempted," as it is written, "when he is drawn away of his own lust and enticed;" "but God tempted no man,"—that is to say, with a hurtful temptation. For temptation is moreover beneficial by which we are not deceived or overwhelmed, but proved, according to that which is said, "Prove me, O Lord, and try me." Therefore, with that hurtful temptation which the apostle signifies when he says, "Lest by some means the tempter have tempted you, and our labor be in vain," "God tempted no man," as I have said, —that is, He brings or leads no one into temptation. For to be tempted and not to be led into temptation is not evil, —nay, it is even good; for this it is to be proved. When, therefore, we say to God, "Lead us not into temptation," what do we say but, "Permit us not to be led"? Whence some pray in this manner, and it is read in many codices, and the most blessed Cyprian thus uses it: "Do not suffer us to be led into temptation." In the Greek gospel, however, I have never found it otherwise than, "Lead us not into temptation." We live, therefore, more securely if we give up the whole to God, and do not entrust ourselves partly to Him and partly to ourselves, as that venerable martyr saw. For when he would expound the same clause of the prayer, he says among other things, "But when we ask that we may not come into temptation, we are reminded of our infirmity and weakness while we thus ask, lest any should insolently vaunt himself,—lest any should proudly and arrogantly assume anything to himself,—lest any should take to himself the glory either of confession or suffering as his own; since the Lord Himself, teaching humility, said, 'Watch and pray, that ye enter not into temptation; the Spirit indeed is willing, but the flesh is weak.' So that when a humble and submissive confession comes first and all is attributed to God, whatever is sought for suppliantly, with the fear of God, may be granted by His own loving-kindness."

Chapter 13 [VII.]—Temptation the Condition of Man.

If, then, there were no other proofs, this Lord's Prayer alone would be sufficient for us on behalf of the grace which I am defending; because it leaves us nothing wherein we may, as it were, glory as in our own, since it shows that our not departing from God is not given except by God, when it shows that it must be asked for from God. For he who is not led into temptation does not depart from God. This is absolutely not in the strength of free will, such as it now is; but it had been in man before he fell. And yet how much this freedom of will availed in the excellence of that primal state appeared in the angels; who, when the devil and his angels fell, stood in the truth, and deserved to attain to that perpetual security of not falling, in which we are most certain that they are now established. But, after the fall of man, God willed it to pertain only to His grace that man should approach to Him; nor did He will it to pertain to aught but His grace that man should not depart from Him.

Chapter 14. —It is God's Grace Both that Man Comes to Him, and that Man Does Not Depart from Him.

This grace He placed "in Him in whom we have obtained a lot, being predestinated according to the purpose of Him who worketh all things." And thus as He worketh that we come to Him, so He worketh that we do not depart. Wherefore it was said to Him by the mouth of the prophet, "Let Thy hand be upon the man of Thy right hand, and upon the Son of man whom Thou made strong for Thyself, and we will not depart from Thee." This certainly is not the first Adam, in whom we departed from Him, but the second Adam, upon whom His hand is placed, so that we do not depart from Him. For Christ altogether with His members is—for the Church's sake, which is His body—the fulness of Him. When, therefore, God's hand is upon Him, that we depart not from God, assuredly God's work reaches to us (for this is God's hand); by which work of God we are caused to be abiding in Christ with God—not, as in Adam, departing from God. For "in Christ we have obtained a lot, being predestinated according to His purpose who worketh all things." This, therefore, is God's hand, not ours, that we depart not from God. That, I say, is His hand who said, "I will put my fear in their hearts, that they depart not from me."

Chapter 15. —Why God Willed that He Should Be Asked for that Which He Might Give Without Prayer.

Wherefore, also He willed that He should be asked that we may not be led into temptation, because if we are not led, we by no means depart from Him. And this might have been given to us even without our praying for it, but by our prayer He willed us to be admonished from whom we receive these benefits. For from whom do we receive but from Him from whom it is right for us to ask? Truly in this matter let not the Church look for laborious disputations but consider its own daily prayers. It prays that the unbelieving may believe; therefore God converts to the faith. It prays that believers may persevere;

therefore, God gives perseverance to the end. God foreknew that He would do this. This is the very predestination of the saints, "whom He has chosen in Christ before the foundation of the world, that they should be holy and unspotted before Him in love; predestinating them unto the adoption of children by Jesus Christ to Himself, according to the good pleasure of His will, to the praise of the glory of His grace, in which He hath shown them favor in His beloved Son, in whom they have redemption through His blood, the forgiveness of sins according to the riches of His grace, which has abounded towards them in all wisdom and prudence; that He might show them the mystery of His will according to His good pleasure which He hath purposed in Him, in the dispensation of the fulness of times to restore all things in Christ which are in heaven and which are in earth; in Him, in whom also we have obtained a lot, being predestinated according to His purpose who worketh all things." Against a trumpet of truth so clear as this, what man of sober and watchful faith can receive any human arguments?

Chapter 16 [VIII.]—Why is Not Grace Given According to Merit?

But "why," says one, "is not the grace of God given according to men's merits?" I answer, Because God is merciful. "Why, then," it is asked, "is it not given to all?" And here I reply, Because God is a Judge. And thus, grace is given by Him freely; and by His righteous judgment it is shown in somewhat grace confers on those to whom it is given. Let us not then be ungrateful, that according to the good pleasure of His will a merciful God delivers so many to the praise of the glory of His grace from such deserved perdition; as, if He should deliver no one therefrom, He would not be unrighteous. Let him, therefore, who is delivered love His grace. Let him who is not delivered acknowledge his due. If, in remitting a debt, goodness is perceived, in requiring it, justice—unrighteousness is never found to be with God.

Chapter 17. —The Difficulty of the Distinction Made in the Choice of One and the Rejection of Another.

"But why," it is said, "in one and the same case, not only of infants, but even of twin children, is the judgment so diverse?" Is it not a similar question, "Why in a different case is the judgment the same?" Let us recall, then, those laborers in the vineyard who worked the whole day, and those who toiled one hour. Certainly, the case was different as to the labor expended, and yet there was the same judgment in paying the wages. Did the murmurers in this case hear anything from the householder except, Such is my will? Certainly, such was his liberality towards some, that there could be no injustice towards others. And both these classes, indeed, are among the good. Nevertheless, so far as it concerns justice and grace, it may be truly said to the guilty who is condemned, also concerning the guilty who is delivered, "Take what thine is, and go thy way;" "I will give unto this one that which is not due;" "Is it not lawful for me to do what I will? is thine eye evil because I am good?" And how if he should say, "Why not to me also?" He will hear, and with reason, "Who art thou, O man, that replies against God?" And although assuredly in the one case you see a most benignant benefactor, and in your own case a most righteous exactor, in neither case do you behold an unjust God. For although He would be righteous even if He were to punish both, he who is delivered has good ground for thankfulness, he who is condemned has no ground for finding fault.

Chapter 18. —But Why Should One Be Punished More Than Another?

"But if," it is said, "it was necessary that, although all were not condemned, He should still show what was due to all, and so He should commend His grace more freely to the vessels of mercy; why in the same case will He punish me more than another, or deliver him more than me?" I say not this. If you ask wherefore; because I confess that I can find no answer to make. And if you further ask why is this, it is because in this matter, even as His anger is righteous and as His mercy is great, so His judgments are unsearchable.

Chapter 19. —Why Does God Mingle Those Who Will Persevere with Those Who Will Not?

Let the inquirer still go on, and say, "Why is it that to some who have in good faith worshipped Him He has not given to persevere to the end?" Why except because he does not speak falsely who says, "They went out from us, but they were not of us; for if they had been of us, doubtless they would have continued with us." Are there, then, two natures of men? By no means. If there were two natures there would not be any grace, for there would be given a gratuitous deliverance to none if it were paid as a debt to nature. But it seems to men that all who appear good believers ought to receive perseverance to the end. But God has judged it to be better to mingle some who would not persevere with a certain number of His saints, so that those for whom security from temptation in this life is not desirable may not be secure. For that which the apostle says, checks many from mischievous elation: "Wherefore let him who seems to stand take heed lest he fall." But he who falls, falls by his own will, and he who stands, stands by God's will. "For God is able to make him stand;" therefore he is not able to make himself stand, but God. Nevertheless, it is good not to be high-minded, but to fear. Moreover, it is in his own thought that everyone either falls or stands. Now, as the apostle says, and as I have mentioned in my former treatise, "We are not sufficient to think anything of ourselves, but our sufficiency is of God." Following whom also the blessed Ambrose ventures to say, "For our heart is not in our own power, nor are our thoughts." And this everybody who is humbly and truly pious feels to be most true.

Chapter 20. —Ambrose on God's Control Over Men's Thoughts.

And when Ambrose said this, he was speaking in that treatise which he wrote concerning Flight from the World, wherein he taught that this world was to be fled not by the body, but by the heart, which he argued could not be done except by God's help. For he says: "We hear frequent discourse concerning fleeing from this world, and I would that the mind was as careful and solicitous as the discourse is easy; but what is worse, the enticement of earthly lusts constantly creeps in, and the pouring out of vanities takes possession of the mind; so that what you desire to avoid, this you think of and consider in your mind. And this is difficult for a man to beware of, but impossible to get rid of. Finally, the prophet bears witness that it is a matter of wish rather than of accomplishment, when he says, 'Incline my heart to Thy testimonies, and not to covetousness.' For our heart and our thoughts are not in our own power, and these, poured forth unexpectedly, confuse our mind and soul, and draw them in a different direction from that which you have proposed to yourself; they recall you to worldly things, they interpose things of time, they suggest voluptuous things, they in weave enticing things, and in the very moment when we are seeking to elevate our mind, we are for the most part filled with vain thoughts and cast down to earthly things." Therefore, it is not in the power of men, but in that of God, that men have power to become sons of God. Because they receive it from Him who gives pious thoughts to the human heart, by which it has faith, which worketh by love; for the receiving and keeping of which benefit, and for carrying it on perseveringly unto the end, we are not sufficient to think anything as of ourselves, but our sufficiency is of God, in whose power is our heart and our thoughts.

Chapter 21 [IX.]—Instances of the Unsearchable Judgments of God.

Therefore, of two infants, equally bound by original sin, why the one is taken and the other left; and of two wicked men of already mature years, why this one should be so called as to follow Him that calleth, while that one is either not called at all, or is not called in such a manner, —the judgments of God are unsearchable. But of two pious men, why to the one should be given perseverance unto the end, and to the other it should not be given, God's judgments are even more unsearchable. Yet to believers it ought to be a most certain fact that the former is of the predestinated, the latter is not. "For if they had been of us," says one of the predestinated, who had drunk this secret from the breast of the Lord, "certainly they would have continued with us." What, I ask, is the meaning of, "They were not of us; for if they had been of us, they would certainly have continued with us"? Were not both created by God—both born of Adam—both made from the earth, and given from Him who said, "I have created all breath," souls of one and the same nature? Lastly, had not both been called, and followed Him that called them? and had not both become, from wicked men, justified men, and both been renewed by the laver of regeneration? But if he were to hear this who beyond all doubt knew what he was saying, he might answer and say: These things are true. In respect of all these things, they were of us. Nevertheless, in respect of a certain other distinction, they were not of us, for if they had been of us, they certainly would have continued with us. What then is this distinction? God's books lie open, let us not turn away our view; the divine Scripture cries aloud, let us give it a hearing. They were not of them, because they had not been "called according to the purpose;" they had not been chosen in Christ before the foundation of the world; they had not gained a lot in Him; they had not been predestinated according to His purpose who worketh all things. For if they had been this, they would have been of them, and without doubt they would have continued with them.

Chapter 22. —It is an Absurdity to Say that the Dead Will Be Judged for Sins Which They Would Have Committed If They Had Lived.

For not to say how possible it may be for God to convert the wills of men averse and opposed to His faith, and to operate on their hearts so that they yield to no adversities, and are overcome by no temptation so as to depart from Him,—since He also can do what the apostle says, namely, not allow them to be tempted above that which they are able;—not, then, to say this, God foreknowing that they would fall, was certainly able to take them away from this life before that fall should occur. Are we to return to that point of still arguing how absurdly it is said that dead men are judged even for those sins which God foreknew that they would have committed if they had lived? which is so abhorrent to the feelings of Christians, or even of human beings, that one is even ashamed to rebut it. Why should it not be said that even the gospel itself has been preached, with so much labor and sufferings of the saints, in vain, or is even still preached in vain, if men could be judged, even without hearing the gospel, according to the contumacy or obedience which God foreknew that they would have had if they had heard it? Tyre and Sidon would not have been condemned, although more slightly than those cities in which, although they did not believe, wonderful works were done by Christ the Lord; because if they had been done in them, they would have repented in dust and ashes, as the utterances of the Truth declare, in which words of His the Lord Jesus shows to us the loftier mystery of predestination.

Chapter 23. —Why for the People of Tyre and Sidon, Who Would Have Believed, the Miracles Were Not Done Which Were Done in Other Places Which Did Not Believe.

For if we are asked why such miracles were done among those who, when they saw them, would not believe them, and were not done among those who would have believed them if they had seen them, what shall we answer? Shall we say what I have said in that book wherein I answered some six questions of the Pagans, yet without prejudice of other matters which the wise can inquire into? This indeed I said, as you know, when it was asked why Christ came after so long a time: "that at those times and in those places in which His gospel was not preached, He foreknew that all men would, in regard of His preaching, be such as many were in His bodily presence,—people, namely, who would not believe on Him, even though the dead were raised by Him." Moreover, a little after in the same book, and on the same question, I say, "What wonder, if Christ knew in former ages that the world was so filled with unbelievers, that He was, with reason, unwilling for His gospel to be preached to them whom He foreknew to be such as would not believe either His words or His miracles"? Certainly, we cannot say this of Tyre and Sidon; and in their case we recognize that those divine judgments had reference to those causes of predestination, without prejudice to which hidden causes I said that I was then answering such questions as those. Certainly, it is easy to accuse the unbelief of the Jews, arising as it did from their free will, since they refused to believe in such great wonders done among themselves. And this the Lord, reproaching them, declares when He says, "Woe unto thee, Chorazin and Bethsaida, because if the mighty works had been done in Tyre and Sidon which have been done in you, they would long ago have repented in dust and ashes." But can we say that even the Tyrians and Sidonians would have refused to believe such mighty works done among them, or would not have believed them if they had been done, when the Lord Himself bears witness to them that they would have repented with great humility if those signs of divine power had been done among them? And yet in the day of judgment they will be punished; although with a less punishment than those cities which would not believe the mighty works done in them. For the Lord goes on to say, "Nevertheless, I say unto you, it shall be more tolerable for Tyre and Sidon in the day of judgment than for you." Therefore, the former shall be punished with greater severity, the latter with less; but yet they shall be punished. Again, if the dead are judged even in respect of deeds which they would have done if they had lived, assuredly since these would have been believers if the gospel had been preached to them with so great miracles, they certainly ought not to be punished; but they will be punished. It is therefore false that the dead are judged in respect also of those things which they would have done if the gospel had reached them when they were alive. And if this is false, there is no ground for saying, concerning infants who perish because they die without baptism, that this happens in their case deservedly, because God foreknew that if they should live and the gospel should be preached to them, they would hear it with unbelief. It remains, therefore, that they are kept bound by original sin alone, and for this alone they go into condemnation; and we see that in others in the same case this is not remitted, except by the gratuitous grace of God in regeneration; and that, by His secret yet righteous judgment—because there is no unrighteousness with God—that some, who even after baptism will perish by evil living, are yet kept in this life until they perish, who would not have perished if bodily death had forestalled their lapse into sin, and so come to their help. Because no dead man is judged by the good or evil things which he would have done if he had not died, otherwise the Tyrians and Sidonians would not have suffered the penalties according to what they did; but rather according to those things that they would have done, if those evangelical mighty works had been done in them, they would have obtained salvation by great repentance, and by the faith of Christ.

Chapter 24 [X.]—It May Be Objected that The People of Tyre and Sidon Might, If They Had Heard, Have Believed, and Have Subsequently Lapsed from Their Faith.

A certain catholic disputant of no mean reputation so expounded this passage of the gospel as to say, that the Lord foreknew that the Tyrians and Sidonians would have afterwards departed from the faith, although they had believed the miracles done among them; and that in mercy He did not work those miracles there, because they would have been liable to severer punishment if they had forsaken the faith which they had once held, than if they had at no time held it. In which opinion of a learned and exceedingly acute man, why am I now concerned to say what is still reasonably to be asked, when even this opinion serves me for the purpose at which I aim? For if the Lord in His mercy did not do mighty works among them, since by these works they might possibly become believers, so that they might not be more severely punished when they should subsequently become unbelievers, as He foreknew that they would,—it is sufficiently and plainly shown that no dead person is judged for those sins which He foreknew that he would have done, if in some manner he were not helped not to do them; just as Christ is said to have come to the aid of the Tyrians and Sidonians, if that opinion be true, who He would rather should not come to the faith at all, than that by a much greater wickedness they should depart from the faith, as, if they had come to it, He foresaw they would have done. Although if it be said, "Why was it not provided that they should rather believe, and this gift should be bestowed on them, that before they forsook the faith they should depart from this life"? I am ignorant what reply can be made. For he who says that to those who would forsake their faith it would have been granted, as a kindness, that they should not begin to have what, by a more serious impiety, they would subsequently forsake, sufficiently indicates that a man is not judged by that which it is foreknown he would have done ill, if by any act of kindness he may be prevented from doing it. Therefore, it is an advantage also to him who is taken away, lest wickedness should alter his understanding. But why this advantage should not have been given to the Tyrians and Sidonians, that they might believe and be taken away, lest wickedness should alter their understanding, he perhaps might answer who was pleased in such a way to solve the above question; but, as far as concerns what I am discussing, I see it to be enough that, even according to that very opinion, men are shown not to be judged in respect of those things which they have not done, even although they may have been foreseen as certain to have done them. However, as I have said, let us think shame even to refute this opinion, whereby sins are supposed to be punished in people who die or have died because they have been foreknown as certain to do them if they had lived; lest we also may seem to have thought it to be of some importance, although we would rather repress it by argument than pass it over in silence.

Chapter 25 [XI.]—God's Ways, Both in Mercy and Judgment, Past Finding Out.

Accordingly, as says the apostle, "It is not of him that wills, nor of him that runs, but of God that shows mercy," who both comes to the help of such infants as He will, although they neither will nor run, since He chose them in Christ before the foundation of the world as those to whom He intended to give His grace freely,—that is, with no merits of theirs, either of faith or of works, preceding; and does not come to the help of those who are more mature, although He foresaw that they would believe His miracles if they should be done among them, because He wills not to come to their help, since in His predestination He, secretly indeed, but yet righteously, has otherwise determined concerning them. For "there is no unrighteousness with God;" but "His judgments are unsearchable, and His ways are past finding out; all the ways of the Lord are mercy and truth." Therefore, the mercy is past finding out by which He has mercy on whom He will, no merits of his own preceding; and the truth is unsearchable by which He hardened whom He will, even although his merits may have preceded, but merits for the most part common to him with the man on whom He has mercy. As of two twins, of which one is taken and the other left, the end is unequal, while the deserts are common, yet in these the one is in such wise delivered by God's great goodness, that the other is condemned by no injustice of God's. For is there unrighteousness with God? Away with the thought! but His ways are past finding out. Therefore, let us believe in His mercy in the case of those who are delivered, and in His truth in the case of those who are punished, without any hesitation; and let us not endeavor to investigate that which is inscrutable, nor to trace that which cannot be found out. Because out of the mouth of babes and sucklings He perfects His praise, so that what we see in those whose deliverance is preceded by no good deservings of theirs, and in those whose condemnation is only preceded by original sin, common alike to both,— this we by no means shrink from as occurring in the case of grown-up people, that is, because we do not think either that grace is given to any one according to his own merits, or that any one is punished except for his own merits, whether they are alike who are delivered and who are punished, or have unequal degrees of evil; so that he who thinks he stands may take heed lest he fall, and he who glories may glory not in himself, but in the Lord.

Chapter 26. —The Manicheans Do Not Receive All the Books of the Old Testament, and of the New Only Those that They Choose.

But wherefore is "the case of infants not allowed," as you write, "to be alleged as an example for their elders," by men who do not hesitate to affirm against the Pelagians that there is original sin, which entered by one man into the world, and that from one all have gone into condemnation? This, the Manicheans, too, do not receive, who not only reject all the Scriptures of the Old Testament as of authority, but even receive those which belong to the New Testament in such a manner as that each man, by his own prerogative as it were, or rather by his own sacrilege, takes what he likes, and rejects what he does not like,—in opposition to whom I treated in my writings on Free Will, whence they think that they have a ground of objection against me. I have been unwilling to deal plainly with the very laborious questions that occurred, lest my work should become too long, in a case which, as opposed to such perverse men, I could not have the assistance of the authority of the sacred Scriptures. And I was able, —as I actually did, whether anything of the divine testimonies might be true or not, seeing that I did not definitely introduce them into the argument, — nevertheless, by certain reasoning, to conclude that God in all things is to be praised, without any necessity of believing, as they would have us, that there are two co-eternal, confounded substances of good and evil.

Chapter 27. —Reference to the "Retractations."

Finally, in the first book of the Retractations, which work of mine you have not yet read, when I had come to the reconsidering of those same books, that is, on the subject of Free Will, I thus spoke: "In these books," I say, "many things were so discussed that on the occurring of some questions which either I was not able to elucidate, or which required a long discussion at once, they were so deferred as that from either side, or from all sides, of those questions in which what was most in harmony with the truth did not appear, yet my reasoning might be conclusive for this, namely, that whichever of them might be true, God might be believed, or even be shown, to be worthy of praise. Because that discussion was undertaken for the sake of those who deny that the origin of evil is derived from the free choice of the will, and contend that God, —if He be so, —as the Creator of all natures, is worthy of blame; desiring in that manner, according to the error of their impiety (for they are Manicheans), to introduce a certain immutable nature of evil co-eternal with God." Also, after a little time, in another place I say: "Then it was said, From this misery, most righteously inflicted on sinners, God's grace delivers, because man of his own accord, that is, by free will, could fall, but could not also rise. To this misery of just condemnation belong the ignorance and the difficulty which every man suffers from the beginning of his birth, and no one is delivered from that evil except by the grace of God. And this misery the Pelagians will not have to descend from a just condemnation, because they deny original sin; although even if the ignorance and difficulty were the natural beginnings of man, God would not even thus deserve to be reproached, but to be praised, as I have argued in the same third book. Which argument must be regarded as against the Manicheans, who do not receive the holy Scriptures of the Old Testament, in which original sin is narrated; and whatever thence is read in the apostolic epistles, they contend was introduced with a detestable impudence by the corrupters of the Scriptures, assuming that it was not said by the apostles. But against the Pelagians that must be maintained which both

Scriptures commend, as they profess to receive them." These things I said in my first book of Retractations, when I was reconsidering the books on Free Will. Nor, indeed, were these things all that were said by me there about these books, but there were many others also, which I thought it would be tedious to insert in this work for you, and not necessary; and this I think you also will judge when you have read all. Although, therefore, in the third book on Free Will I have in such wise argued concerning infants, that even if what the Pelagians say were true, —that ignorance and difficulty, without which no man is born, are elements, not punishments, of our nature, —still the Manicheans would be overcome, who will have it that the two natures, to wit, of good and evil, are co-eternal. Is, therefore, the faith to be called in question or forsaken, which the catholic Church maintains against those very Pelagians, asserting as she does that it is original sin, the guilt of which, contracted by generation, must be remitted by regeneration? And if they confess this with us, so that we may at once, in this matter of the Pelagians, destroy error, why do they think that it must be doubted that God can deliver even infants, to whom He gives His grace by the sacrament of baptism, from the power of darkness, and translate them into the kingdom of the Son of His love? In the fact, therefore, that He gives that grace to some, and does not give it to others, why will they not sing to the Lord His mercy and judgment? Why, however, is it given to these, rather than to those, —who has known the mind of the Lord? who is able to investigate unsearchable things? who to trace out that which is past finding out?

Chapter 28 [XII.]—God's Goodness and Righteousness Shown in All.

It is therefore settled that God's grace is not given according to the deserts of the recipients, but according to the good pleasure of His will, to the praise and glory of His own grace; so that he who glories may by no means glory in himself, but in the Lord, who gives to those men to whom He will, because He is merciful, what if, however, He does not give, He is righteous: and He does not give to whom He will not, that He may make known the riches of His glory to the vessels of mercy. For by giving to some what they do not deserve, He has certainly willed that His grace should be gratuitous, and thus genuine grace; by not giving to all, He has shown what all deserve. Good in His goodness to some, righteous in the punishment of others; both good in respect of all, because it is good when that which is due is rendered, and righteous in respect of all, since that which is not due is given without wrong to anyone.

Chapter 29. —God's True Grace Could Be Defended Even If There Were No Original Sin, as Pelagius Maintains.

But God's grace, that is, true grace without merits, is maintained, even if infants, when baptized, according to the view of the Pelagians, are not plucked out of the power of darkness, because they are held guilty of no sin, as the Pelagians think, but are only transferred into the Lord's kingdom: for even thus, without any good merits, the kingdom is given to those to whom it is given; and without any evil merits it is not given to them to whom it is not given. And this we are in the habit of saying in opposition to the same Pelagians, when they object to us that we attribute God's grace to fate, when we say that it is given not in respect to our merits. For they themselves rather attribute God's grace to fate in the case of infants, if they say that when there is no merit it is fate. Certainly, even according to the Pelagians themselves, no merits can be found in infants to cause that some of them should be admitted into the kingdom, and others should be alienated from the kingdom. But now, just as in order to show that God's grace is not given according to our merits, I preferred to maintain this truth in accordance with both opinions,—both in accordance with our own, to wit, who say that infants are bound by original sin, and according to that of the Pelagians, who deny that there is original sin, and yet I cannot on that account doubt that infants have what He can pardon them who saves His people from their sins: so in the third book on Free Will, according to both views, I have withstood the Manicheans, whether ignorance and difficulty be punishments or elements of nature without which no man is born; and yet I hold one of these views. There, moreover, it is sufficiently evidently declared by me, that that is not the nature of man as he was ordained, but his punishment as condemned.

Chapter 30. —Augustin Claims the Right to Grow in Knowledge.

Therefore, it is in vain that it is prescribed to me from that old book of mine, that I may not argue the case as I ought to argue it in respect of infants; and that thence I may not persuade my opponents by the light of a manifest truth, that God's grace is not given according to men's merits. For if, when I began my books concerning Free Will as a layman, and finished them as a presbyter, I still doubted of the condemnation of infants not born again, and of the deliverance of infants that were born again, no one, as I think, would be so unfair and envious as to hinder my progress, and judge that I must continue in that uncertainty. But it can more correctly be understood that it ought to be believed that I did not doubt in that matter, for the reason that they against whom my purpose was directed seemed to me in such wise to be rebutted, as that whether there was a punishment of original sin in infants, according to the truth, or whether there was not, as some mistaken people think, yet in no degree should such a confusion of the two natures be believed in, to wit, of good and evil, as the error of the Manicheans introduces. Be it therefore far from us so to forsake the case of infants as to say to ourselves that it is uncertain whether, being regenerated in Christ, if they die in infancy they pass into eternal salvation; but that, not being regenerated, they pass into the second death. Because that which is written, "By one man sin entered into the world, and death by sin, and so death passed upon all men," cannot be rightly understood in any other manner; nor from that eternal death which is most righteously repaid to sin does any deliver any one, small or great, save He who, for the sake of remitting our sins, both original and personal, died without any sin of His own, either original or personal. But why some rather than others? Again, and again we say, and do not shrink from it, "O man, who art thou that replies against God?" "His judgments are unsearchable, and His ways past finding out." And let us add this, "Seek not out the things that are too high for thee, and search not the things that are above thy strength."

Chapter 31. —Infants are Not Judged According to that Which They are Foreknown as Likely to Do If They Should Live.

For you see, beloved, how absurd it is, and how foreign from soundness of faith and sincerity of truth, for us to say that infants, when they die, should be judged according to those things which they are foreknown to be going to do if they should live. For to this opinion, from which certainly every human feeling, on however little reason it may be founded, and especially every Christian feeling, revolts, they are compelled to advance who have chosen in such wise to be withdrawn from the error of the Pelagians as still to think that they must believe, and, moreover, must profess in argument, that the grace of God, through Jesus Christ our Lord, by which alone after the fall of the first man, in whom we all fell, help is afforded to us, is given according to our merits. And this belief Pelagius himself, before the Eastern bishops as judges, condemned in fear of his own condemnation. And if this be not said of the good or bad works of those who have died, which they would have done if they had lived,—and thus of no works, and works that would never exist, even in the foreknowledge of God,—if this, therefore, be not said, and you see under how great a mistake it is said, what will remain but that we confess, when the darkness of contention is removed, that the grace of God is not given according to our merits, which position the catholic Church defends against the Pelagian heresy; and that we see this in more evident truth especially in infants? For God is not compelled by fate to come to the help of these infants, and not to come to the help of those, —since the case is alike to both. Or shall we think that human affairs in the case of infants are not managed by Divine Providence, but by fortuitous chances, when rational souls are either to be condemned or delivered, although, indeed, not a sparrow falls to the ground without the will of our Father which is in heaven? Or must we so attribute it to the negligence of parents that infants die without baptism, as that heavenly judgments have nothing to do with it; as if they themselves who in this way die badly had of their own will chosen the negligent parents for themselves of whom they were born? What shall I say when an infant expires some time before he can possibly be advantaged by the ministry of baptism? For often when the parents are eager, and the ministers prepared for giving baptism to the infants, it still is not given, because God does not choose; since He has not kept it in this life for a little while in order that baptism might be given it. What, moreover, when sometimes aid could be afforded by baptism to the children of unbelievers, that they should not go into perdition, and could not be afforded to the children of believers? In which case it is certainly shown that there is no acceptance of persons with God; otherwise He would rather deliver the children of His worshippers than the children of His enemies.

Chapter 32 [XIII.]—The Inscrutability of God's Free Purposes.

But now, since we are now treating of the gift of perseverance, why is it that aid is afforded to the person about to die who is not baptized, while to the baptized person about to fall, aid is not afforded, so as to die before? Unless, perchance, we shall still listen to that absurdity by which it is said that it is of no advantage to anyone to die before his fall, because he will be judged according to those actions which God foreknew that he would have done if he had lived. Who can hear with patience this perversity, so violently opposed to the soundness of the faith? Who can bear it? And yet they are driven to say this who do not confess that God's grace is not bestowed in respect of our deservings. They, however, who will not say that anyone who has died is judged according to those things which God foreknew that he would have done if he had lived, considering with how manifest a falsehood and how great an absurdity this would be said, have no further reason to say, what the Church condemned in the Pelagians, and caused to be condemned by Pelagius himself,—that the grace of God, namely, is given according to our merits,—when they see some infants not regenerated taken from this life to eternal death, and others regenerated, to eternal life; and those themselves that are regenerated, some going hence, persevering even to the end, and others kept in this life even until they fall, who certainly would not have fallen if they had departed hence before their lapse; and again some falling, but not departing from this life until they return, who certainly would have perished if they had departed before their return.

Chapter 33. —God Gives Both Initiatory and Persevering Grace According to His Own Will.

From all which it is shown with sufficient

clearness that the grace of God, which both begins a man's faith and which enables it to persevere unto the end, is not given according to our merits, but is given according to His own most secret and at the same time most righteous, wise, and beneficent will; since those whom He predestinated, them He also called, with that calling of which it is said, "The gifts and calling of God are without repentance." To which calling there is no man that can be said by men with any certainty of affirmation to belong, until he has departed from this world; but in this life of man, which is a state of trial upon the earth, he who seems to stand must take heed lest he fall. Since (as I have already said before) those who will not persevere are, by the most foreseeing will of God, mingled with those who will persevere, because we may learn not to mind high things, but to consent to the lowly, and may "work out our own salvation with fear and trembling; for it is God that worketh in us both to will and to do for His good pleasure." We therefore will, but God worketh in us to will also. We therefore work, but God worketh in us to work also for His good pleasure. This is profitable for us both to believe and to say, —this is pious, this is true, that our confession be lowly and submissive, and that all should be given to God. Thinking, we believe; thinking, we speak; thinking, we do whatever we do; but, in respect of what concerns the way of piety and the true worship of God, we are not sufficient to think anything as of ourselves, but our sufficiency is of God. For "our heart and our thoughts are not in our own power;" whence the same Ambrose who says this says also: "But who is so blessed as in his heart always to rise upwards? And how can this be done without divine help? Assuredly, by no means. Finally," he says, "the same Scripture affirms above, 'Blessed is the man whose help is of Thee; O Lord, ascent is in his heart.'" Assuredly, Ambrose was not only enabled to say this by reading in the holy writings, but as of such a man is to be without doubt believed, he felt it also in his own heart. Therefore, as is said in the sacraments of believers, that we should lift up our hearts to the Lord, is God's gift; for which gift they to whom this is said are admonished by the priest after this word to give thanks to our Lord God Himself; and they answer that it is "meet and right so to do." For, since our heart is not in our own power, but is lifted up by the divine help, so that it ascends and takes cognizance of those things which are above, where Christ is sitting at the right hand of God, and, not those things that are upon the earth, to whom are thanks to be given for so great a gift as this unless to our Lord God who doeth this,—who in so great kindness has chosen us by delivering us from the abyss of this world, and has predestinated us before the foundation of the world?

Chapter 34 [XIV.]—The Doctrine of Predestination Not Opposed to the Advantage of Preaching.

But they say that the "definition of predestination is opposed to the advantage of preaching,"—as if, indeed, it were opposed to the preaching of the apostle! Did not that teacher of the heathen so often, in faith and truth, both commend predestination, and not cease to preach the word of God? Because he said, "It is God that worketh in you both to will and to do for His good pleasure," did he not also exhort that we should both will and do what is pleasing to God? or because he said, "He who hath begun a good work in you shall carry it on even unto the day of Christ Jesus," did he on that account cease to persuade men to begin and to persevere unto the end? Doubtless, our Lord Himself commanded men to believe, and said, "Believe in God, believe also in me:" and yet His opinion is not therefore false, nor is His definition idle when He says, "No man cometh unto me"—that is, no man believeth in me— "except it has been given him of my Father." Nor, again, because this definition is true, is the former precept vain. Why, therefore, do we think the definition of predestination useless to preaching, to precept, to exhortation, to rebuke, —all which things the divine Scripture repeats frequently, —seeing that the same Scripture commends this doctrine?

Chapter 35. —What Predestination is.

Will any man dare to say that God did not foreknow those to whom He would give to believe, or whom He would give to His Son, that of them He should lose none? And certainly, if He foreknew these things, He as certainly foreknew His own kindnesses, wherewith He condescends to deliver us. This is the predestination of the saints, —nothing else; to wit, the foreknowledge and the preparation of God's kindnesses, whereby they are most certainly delivered, whoever they are that are delivered. But where are the rest left by the righteous divine judgment except in the mass of ruin, where the Tyrians and the Sidonians were left? who, moreover, might have believed if they had seen Christ's wonderful miracles. But since it was not given to them to believe, the means of believing also were denied them. From which fact it appears that some have in their understanding itself a naturally divine gift of intelligence, by which they may be moved to the faith, if they either hear the words or behold the signs congruous to their minds; and yet if, in the higher judgment of God, they are not by the predestination of grace separated from the mass of perdition, neither those very divine words nor deeds are applied to them by which they might believe if they only heard or saw such things. Moreover, in the same mass of ruin the Jews were left, because they could not believe such great and eminent mighty works as were done in their sight. For the gospel has not been silent about the reason why they could not believe, since it says: "But though He had done such great miracles before them, yet they believed not on Him; that the saying of Isaiah the prophet might be fulfilled which he spoke, Lord, who hath believed our report, and to whom hath the arm of the Lord been revealed? And, therefore, they could not believe, because that Isaiah said again, He hath blinded their eyes and hardened their heart, that they should not see with their eyes, nor understand with their heart, and be converted, and I should heal them." Therefore, the eyes of the Tyrians and Sidonians were not so blinded nor was their heart so hardened, since they would have believed if they had seen such mighty works, as the Jews saw. But it did not profit them that they were able to believe, because they were not predestinated by Him whose judgments are inscrutable and His ways past finding out. Neither would inability to believe have been a hindrance to them, if they had been so predestinated as that God should illuminate those blind eyes and should will to take away the stony heart from those hardened ones. But what the Lord said of the Tyrians and Sidonians may perchance be understood in another way: that no one nevertheless comes to Christ unless it were given him, and that it is given to those who are chosen in Him before the foundation of the world, he confesses beyond a doubt who hears the divine utterance, not with the deaf ears of the flesh, but with the ears of the heart; and yet this predestination, which is plainly enough unfolded even by the words of the gospels, did not prevent the Lord's saying as well in respect of the commencement, what I have a little before mentioned, "Believe in God; believe also in me," as in respect of perseverance, "A man ought always to pray, and not to faint." For they hear these things and do them to whom it is given; but they do them not, whether they hear or do not hear, to whom it is not given. Because, "To you," said He, "it is given to know the mystery of the kingdom of heaven, but to them it is not given." Of these, the one refers to the mercy, the other to the judgment of Him to whom our soul cries, "I will sing of mercy and judgment unto Thee, O Lord."

Chapter 36. —The Preaching of the Gospel and the Preaching of Predestination the Two Parts of One Message.

Therefore, by the preaching of predestination, the preaching of a persevering and progressive faith is not to be hindered; and thus they may hear what is necessary to whom it is given that they should obey. For how shall they hear without a preacher? Neither, again, is the preaching of a progressive faith which continues even to the end to hinder the preaching of predestination, so that he who is living faithfully and obediently may not be lifted up by that very obedience, as if by a benefit of his own, not received; but that he that glories may glory in the Lord. For "we must boast in nothing, since nothing is our own." And this, Cyprian most faithfully saw and most fearlessly explained, and thus he pronounced predestination to be most assured. For if we must boast in nothing, seeing that nothing is our own, certainly we must not boast of the most persevering obedience. Nor is it so to be called our own, as if it were not given to us from above. And, therefore, it is God's gift, which, by the confession of all Christians, God foreknew that He would give to His people, who were called by that calling whereof it was said, "The gifts and calling of God are without repentance." This, then, is the predestination which we faithfully and humbly preach. Nor yet did the same teacher and doer, who both believed on Christ and most perseveringly lived in holy obedience, even to suffering for Christ, cease on that account to preach the gospel, to exhort to faith and to pious manners, and to that very perseverance to the end, because he said, "We must boast in nothing, since nothing is our own;" and here he declared without ambiguity the true grace of God, that is, that which is not given in respect of our merits; and since God foreknew that He would give it, predestination was announced beyond a doubt by these words of Cyprian; and if this did not prevent Cyprian from preaching obedience, it certainly ought not to prevent us.

Chapter 37. —Ears to Hear are a Willingness to Obey.

Although, therefore, we say that obedience is the gift of God, we still exhort men to it. But to those who obediently hear the exhortation of truth is given the gift of God itself—that is, to hear obediently; while to those who do not thus hear it is not given. For it was not someone only, but Christ who said, "No man cometh unto me, except it were given him of my Father;" and, "To you it is given to know the mystery of the kingdom of heaven, but to them it is not given." And concerning continence He says, "Not all receive this saying, but they to whom it is given." And when the apostle would exhort married people to conjugal chastity, he says, "I would that all men were even as I myself; but every man hath his proper gift of God, one after this manner, another after that;" where he plainly shows not only that continence is a gift of God, but even the chastity of those who are married. And although these things are true, we still exhort to them as much as is given to any one of us to be able to exhort, because this also is His gift in whose hand are both ourselves and our discourses. Whence also says the apostle, "According to this grace of God which is given unto me, as a wise architect, I have laid the foundation." And in another place he says, "Even as the Lord hath given to every man: I have planted, Apollos has watered, but God has given the increase. Therefore, neither is he that planted anything, nor he that watered, but God that giveth the increase." And thus, as only he preaches and exhorts rightly who has received this gift, so assuredly he who obediently hears him who rightly exhorts and preaches is he who has received this gift. Hence is what the Lord said, when, speaking to those who had their fleshly ears open, He nevertheless told them, "He that hath ears to hear let him hear;" which beyond a doubt he knew that not all had. And from whom they have, whosoever they be that have them, the Lord Himself shows when He says, "I will give them a heart to know me, and ears to hear." Therefore, having ears is itself the gift of obeying, so that they who had that came to Him, to whom "no one comes unless it were given to him of His Father." Therefore we exhort and preach, but they who have ears to hear obediently hear us, while in them who have them not, it comes to pass what is written, that hearing they do not hear, —hearing, to wit, with the bodily sense, they do not hear with the assent of the heart. But why these should have ears to hear, and those have them not, —that is, why to these it should be given by the Father to come to the Son, while to those it should not be given, —who has known the mind of the Lord, or who has been His counsellor? Or who art thou, O man, that replies against God? Must that which is manifest be denied, because that which is hidden cannot be comprehended? Shall we, I say, declare that what we see to be so is not so, because we cannot find out why it is so?

Chapter 38 [XV.]—Against the Preaching of Predestination the Same Objections May Be Alleged as Against Predestination.

But they say, as you write: "That no one can be aroused by the incentives of rebuke if it be said in the assembly of the Church to the multitude of hearers: The definite meaning of God's will concerning predestination stands in such wise, that some of you will receive the will to obey and will come out of unbelief unto faith, or will receive perseverance and abide in the faith; but others who are lingering in the delight of sins have not yet arisen, for the reason that the aid of pitying grace has not yet indeed raised you up. But yet, if there are any whom by His grace He has predestinated to be chosen, who are not yet called, ye shall receive that grace by which you may will and be chosen; and if any obey, if ye are predestinated to be rejected, the strength to obey shall be withdrawn from you, so that you may cease to obey." Although these things may be said, they ought not so to deter us from confessing the true grace of God,—that is, the grace which is not given to us in respect of our merits,—and from confessing the predestination of the saints in accordance therewith, even as we are not deterred from confessing God's foreknowledge, although one should thus speak to the people concerning it, and say: "Whether you are now living righteously or unrighteously, you shall be such by and by as the Lord has foreknown that you will be,—either good, if He has foreknown you as good, or bad, if He has foreknown you as bad." For if on the hearing of this some should be turned to torpor and slothfulness, and from striving should go headlong to lust after their own desires, is it therefore to be counted that what has been said about the foreknowledge of God is false? If God has foreknown that they will be good, will they not be good, whatever be the depth of evil in which they are now engaged? And if He has foreknown them evil, will they not be evil, whatever goodness may now be discerned in them? There was a man in our monastery, who, when the brethren rebuked him for doing some things that ought not to be done, and for not doing some things that ought to be done, replied, "Whatever I may now be, I shall be such as God has foreknown that I shall be." And this man certainly both said what was true, and was not profited by this truth for good, but so far made way in evil as to desert the society of the monastery, and become a dog returned to his vomit; and, nevertheless, it is uncertain what he is yet to become. For the sake of souls of this kind, then, is the truth which is spoken about God's foreknowledge either to be denied or to be kept back, —at such times, for instance, when, if it is not spoken, other errors are incurred?

Chapter 39 [XVI]—Prayer and Exhortation.

There are some, moreover, who either do not pray at all, or pray coldly, because, from the Lord's words, they have learnt that God knows what is necessary for us before we ask it of Him. Must the truth of this declaration be given up, or shall we think that it should be erased from the gospel because of such people? Nay, since it is manifest that God has prepared some things to be given even to those who do not pray for them, such as the beginning of faith, and other things not to be given except to those who pray for them, such as perseverance even unto the end, certainly he who thinks that he has this latter from himself does not pray to have it. Therefore we must take care lest, while we are afraid of exhortation growing lukewarm, prayer should be stifled and arrogance stimulated.

Chapter 40. —When the Truth Must Be Spoken, When Kept Back.

Therefore let the truth be spoken, especially when any question impels us to declare it; and let them receive it who are able, lest, perchance, while we are silent because of those who cannot receive it, they be not only defrauded of the truth but be taken captive by falsehood, who are able to receive the truth whereby falsehood may be avoided. For it is easy, nay, and it is useful, that some truth should be kept back because of those who are incapable of apprehending it. For whence is that word of our Lord: "I have yet many things to say unto you, but ye cannot bear them now"? And that of the apostle: "I could not speak unto you as unto spiritual, but as unto carnal: as if unto babes in Christ I have given you to drink milk, and not meat, for hitherto ye were not able, neither yet indeed now are ye able"? Although, in a certain manner of speaking, it might happen that what is said should be both milk to infants and meat for grown-up persons. As "in the beginning was the Word, and the Word was with God, and the Word was God," what Christian can keep it back? Who can receive it? Or what in sound doctrine can be found more comprehensive? And yet this is not kept back either from infants or from grown-up people, nor is it hidden from infants by those who are mature. But the reason of keeping back the truth is one, the necessity of speaking the truth is another. It would be a tedious business to inquire into or to put down all the reasons for keeping back the truth; of which, nevertheless, there is this one, —lest we should make those who do not understand worse, while wishing to make those who do understand more learned; although these latter do not become more learned when we withhold any such thing on the one hand, but also do not become worse. When, however, a truth is of such a nature that he who cannot receive it is made worse by our speaking it, and he who can receive it is made worse by our silence concerning it, what do we think is to be done? Must we not speak the truth, that he who can receive it may receive it, rather than keep silence, so that not only neither may receive it, but that even he who is more intelligent should himself be made worse? For if he should hear and receive it, by his means also many might learn. For in proportion as he is more capable of learning, he is the more fitted for teaching others. The enemy of grace presses on and urges in all ways to make us believe that grace is given according to our deservings, and thus grace is no more grace; and are we unwilling to say what we can say by the testimony of Scripture? Do we fear, forsooth, to offend by our speaking him who is not able to receive the truth? and are we not afraid lest by our silence he who can receive the truth may be involved in falsehood?

Chapter 41. —Predestination Defined as Only God's Disposing of Events in His Foreknowledge.

For either predestination must be preached, in the way and degree in which the Holy Scripture plainly declares it, so that in the predestinated the gifts and calling of God may be without repentance; or it must be avowed that God's grace is given according to our merits,—which is the opinion of the Pelagians; although that opinion of theirs, as I have often said already, may be read in the Proceedings of the Eastern bishops to have been condemned by the lips of Pelagius himself. Further, those on whose account I am discoursing are only removed from the heretical perversity of the Pelagians, inasmuch as, although they will not confess that they who by God's grace are made obedient and so abide, are predestinated, they still confess, nevertheless, that this grace precedes their will to whom it is given; in such a way certainly as that grace may not be thought to be given freely, as the truth declares, but rather according to the merits of a preceding will, as the Pelagian error says, in contradiction to the truth. Therefore, also, grace precedes faith; otherwise, if faith precedes grace, beyond a doubt will also precedes it, because there cannot be faith without will. But if grace precedes faith because it precedes will, certainly it precedes all obedience; it also precedes love, by which alone God is truly and pleasantly obeyed. And all these things grace works in him to whom it is given, and in whom it precedes all these things. [XVII.] Among these benefits there remains perseverance unto the end, which is daily asked for in vain from the Lord, if the Lord by His grace does not affect it in him whose prayers He hears. See now how foreign it is from the truth to deny that perseverance even to the end of this life is the gift of God; since He Himself puts an end to this life when He wills, and if He puts an end before a fall that is threatening, He makes the man to persevere even unto the end. But more marvelous and more manifest to believers is the largess of God's goodness, that this grace is given even to infants, although there is no obedience at that age to which it may be given. To whomsoever, therefore, God gives His gifts, beyond a doubt He has foreknown that He will bestow them on them, and in His foreknowledge He has prepared them for them. Therefore, those whom He predestinated, them He also called with that calling which I am not reluctant often to make mention of, of which it is said, "The gifts and calling of God are without repentance." For the ordering of His future works in His foreknowledge, which cannot be deceived and changed, is absolute, and is nothing but, predestination. But, as he whom God has foreknown to be chaste, although he may regard it as uncertain, so acts as to be chaste, so he whom He has predestinated to be chaste, although he may regard that as uncertain, does not, therefore, fail to act so as to be chaste because he hears that he is to be what he will be by the gift of God. Nay, rather, his love rejoices, and he is not puffed up as if he had not received it. Not only, therefore, is he not hindered from this work by the preaching of predestination, but he is even assisted to it, so that although he glories he may glory in the Lord.

Chapter 42. —The Adversaries Cannot Deny Predestination to Those Gifts of Grace Which They Themselves Acknowledge, and Their Exhortations are Not Hindered by This Predestination Nevertheless.

And what I said of chastity, can be said also of faith, of piety, of love, of perseverance, and, not to enumerate single virtues, it may be said with the utmost truthfulness of all the obedience with which God is obeyed. But those who place only the beginning of faith and perseverance to the end in such wise in our power as not to regard them as God's gifts, nor to think that God works on our thoughts and wills so as that we may have and retain them, grant, nevertheless, that He gives other things, —since they are obtained from Him by the faith of the believer. Why are they not afraid that exhortation to these other things, and the preaching of these other things, should be hindered by the definition of predestination? Or, perchance, do they say that such things are not predestinated? Then they are not given by God, or He has not known that He would give them. Because, if they are both given, and He foreknew that He would give them, certainly He predestinated them. As, therefore, they themselves also exhort to chastity, charity, piety, and other things which they confess to be God's gifts, and cannot deny that they are also foreknown by Him, and therefore predestinated; nor do they say that their exhortations are hindered by the preaching of God's predestination, that is, by the preaching of God's foreknowledge of those future gifts of His: so they may see that neither are their exhortations to faith or to perseverance hindered, even although those very things may be said, as is the truth, to be gifts of God, and that those things are foreknown, that is, predestinated to be given; but let them rather see that by this preaching of predestination only that most pernicious error is hindered and overthrown, whereby it is said that the grace of God is given according to our deservings, so that he who glories may glory not in the Lord, but in himself.

Chapter 43. —Further Development of the Foregoing Argument.

And in order that I may more openly unfold this for the sake of those who are somewhat slow of apprehension, let those who are endowed with an intelligence that flies in advance bear with my delay. The Apostle James says, "If any of you lack wisdom, let him ask of God, who giveth to all men liberally and upbraided not, and it shall be given him." It is written also in the Proverbs of Solomon, "Because the Lord giveth wisdom." And of continency it is read in the book of Wisdom, whose authority has been used by great and learned men who have commented upon the divine utterances long before us; there, therefore, it is read, "When I knew that no one can be continent unless God gives it, and that this was of wisdom, to know whose gift this was." Therefore these are God's gifts, —that is, to say nothing of others, wisdom and continency. Let those also acquiesce: for they are not Pelagians, to contend against such a manifest truth as this with hard and heretical perversity. "But," say they, "that these things are given to us of God is obtained by faith, which has its beginning from us;" and both to begin to have this faith, and to abide in it even to the end, they contend is our own doing, as if we received it not from the Lord. This, beyond a doubt, is in contradiction to the apostle when he says, "For what hast thou that thou hast not received?" It is in contradiction also to the saying of the martyr Cyprian, "That we must boast in nothing, since nothing is our own." When we have said this, and many other things which it is wearisome to repeat, and have shown that both the commencement of faith and perseverance to the end are gifts of God; and that it is impossible that God should not foreknow any of His future gifts, as well what should be given as to whom they should be given; and that thus those whom He delivers and crowns are predestinated by Him; they think it well to reply, "that the assertion of predestination is opposed to the advantage of preaching, for the reason that when this is heard no one can be stirred up by the incentives of rebuke." When they say this, "they are unwilling that it should be declared to men, that coming to the faith and abiding in the faith are God's gifts, lest despair rather than encouragement should appear to be suggested, inasmuch as they who hear think that it is uncertain to human ignorance on whom God bestows, or on whom He does not bestow, these gifts." Why, then, do they themselves also preach with us that wisdom and continency are God's gifts? But if, when these things are declared to be God's gifts, there is no hindrance of the exhortation with which we exhort men to be wise and continent; what is after all the reason for their thinking that the exhortation is hindered wherewith we exhort men to come to the faith, and to abide in it to the end, if these also are said to be

God's gifts, as is proved by the Scriptures, which are His witnesses?

Chapter 44. —Exhortation to Wisdom, Though Wisdom is God's Gift.

Now, to say nothing more of continency, and to argue in this place of wisdom alone, certainly the Apostle James above mentioned says, "But the wisdom that is from above is first pure, then peaceable, modest, easy to be entreated, full of mercy and good fruits, inestimable, without simulation." Do you not see, I beseech you, how this wisdom descends from the Father of Lights, laden with many and great benefits? Because, as the same apostle says, "Every excellent gift and every perfect gift is from above and comes down from the Father of Lights." Why, then—to set aside other matters—do we rebuke the impure and contentious, to whom we nevertheless preach that the gift of God is wisdom, pure and peaceable; and are not afraid that they should be influenced, by the uncertainty of the divine will, to find in this preaching more of despair than of exhortation; and that they should not be stirred up by the incentives of rebuke rather against us than against themselves, because we rebuke them for not having those things which we ourselves say are not produced by human will, but are given by the divine liberality? Finally, why did the preaching of this grace not deter the Apostle James from rebuking restless souls, and saying, "If ye have bitter envying, and contentions are in your hearts, glory not, and be not liars against the truth. This is not the wisdom that cometh down from above, but is earthly, animal, devilish; for where envying and contention are, there are inconstancy and every evil work"? As, therefore, the restless are to be rebuked, both by the testimony of the divine declarations, and by those very impulses of ours which they have in common with ourselves; and is it no argument against this rebuke that we declare the peaceful wisdom, whereby the contentions are corrected and healed, to be the gift of God; unbelievers are in such wise to be rebuked, as those who do not abide in the faith, without any hindrance to that rebuke from the preaching of God's grace, although that preaching commends that very grace and the continuance in it as the gifts of God. Because, although wisdom is obtained from faith, even as James himself, when he had said, "If any of you lack wisdom, let him ask of God, who giveth to all liberally and upbraided not, and it shall be given," immediately added, "But let him ask in faith, nothing wavering:" it is not, nevertheless, because faith is given before it is asked for by him to whom it is given, that it must therefore be said not to be the gift of God, but to be of ourselves, because it is given to us without our asking for it! For the apostle very plainly says, "Peace be to the brethren, and love with faith from God the Father and the Lord Jesus Christ." From whom, therefore, are peace and love, from Him also is faith; wherefore, from Him we ask not only that it may be increased to those that possess it, but also that it may be given to those that possess it not.

Chapter 45. —Exhortation to Other Gifts of God in Like Manner.

Nor do those on whose account I am saying these things, who cry out that exhortation is checked by the preaching of predestination and grace, exhort to those gifts alone which they contend are not given by God, but are from ourselves, such as are the beginning of faith, and perseverance in it even to the end. This certainly they ought to do, in such a way as only to exhort unbelievers to believe, and believers to continue to believe. But those things which with us they do not deny to be God's gifts, so as that with us they demolish the error of the Pelagians, such as modesty, continence, patience, and other virtues that pertain to a holy life, and are obtained by faith from the Lord, they ought to show as needing to be prayed for, and to pray for only, either for themselves or others; but they ought not to exhort any one to strive after them and retain them. But when they exhort to these things, according to their ability, and confess that men ought to be exhorted, —certainly they show plainly enough that exhortations are not hindered by that preaching, whether they are exhortations to faith or to perseverance to the end, because we also preach that such things are God's gifts, and are not given by any man to himself, but are given by God.

Chapter 46. —A Man Who Does Not Persevere Fails by His Own Fault.

But it is said, "It is by his own fault that any one deserts the faith, when he yields and consents to the temptation which is the cause of his desertion of the faith." Who denies it? But because of this, perseverance in the faith is not to be said not to be a gift of God. For it is this that a man daily asks for when he says, "Lead us not into temptation;" and if he is heard, it is this that he receives. And thus as he daily asks for perseverance, he assuredly places the hope of his perseverance not in himself, but in God. I, however, am loth to exaggerate the case with my words, but I rather leave it to them to consider, and see what it is of which they have persuaded themselves—to wit, "that by the preaching of predestination, more of despair than of exhortation is impressed upon the hearers." For this is to say that a man then despairs of his salvation when he has learned to place his hope not in himself, but in God, although the prophet cries, "Cursed is he who has his hope in man."

Chapter 47. —Predestination is Sometimes Signified Under the Name of Foreknowledge.

These gifts, therefore, of God, which are given to the elect who are called according to God's purpose, among which gifts is both the beginning of belief and perseverance in the faith to the termination of this life, as I have proved by such a concurrent testimony of reasons and authorities, —these gifts of God, I say, if there is no such predestination as I am maintaining, are not foreknown by God. But they are foreknown. This, therefore, is the predestination which I maintain. [XVIII.] Consequently, sometimes the same predestination is signified also under the name of foreknowledge; as says the apostle, "God has not rejected His people whom He foreknew." Here, when he says, "He foreknew," the sense is not rightly understood except as "He predestinated," as is shown by the context of the passage itself. For he was speaking of the remnant of the Jews which were saved, while the rest perished. For above he had said that the prophet had declared to Israel, "All day long I have stretched forth my hands to an unbelieving and a gainsaying people." And as if it were answered, What, then, has become of the promises of God to Israel? he added in continuation, "I say, then, has God cast away His people? God forbid! for I also am an Israelite, of the seed of Abraham, of the tribe of Benjamin." Then he added the words which I am now treating: "God hath not cast away His people whom He foreknew." And in order to show that the remnant had been left by God's grace, not by any merits of their works, he went on to add, "Know ye not what the Scripture saith in Elias, in what way he makes intercession with God against Israel?" and the rest. "But what," says he, "saith the answer of God unto him? 'I have reserved to myself seven thousand men, who have not bowed the knee before Baal.'" For He says not, "There are left to me," or "They have reserved themselves to me," but, "I have reserved to myself." "Even so, then, at this present time also there is made a remnant by the election of grace. And if of grace, then it is no more by works; otherwise grace is no more grace." And connecting this with what I have above quoted, "What then?" and in answer to this inquiry, he says, "Israel hath not obtained that which he was seeking for, but the election hath obtained it, and the rest were blinded." Therefore, in the election, and in this remnant which were made so by the election of grace, he wished to be understood the people which God did not reject, because He foreknew them. This is that election by which He elected those, whom He willed, in Christ before the foundation of the world, that they should be holy and without spot in His sight, in love, predestinating them unto the adoption of sons. No one, therefore, who understands these things is permitted to doubt that, when the apostle says, "God hath not cast away His people whom He foreknew," He intended to signify predestination. For He foreknew the remnant which He should make so according to the election of grace. That is, therefore, He predestinated them; for without doubt He foreknew if He predestinated; but to have predestinated is to have foreknown that which He should do.

Chapter 48 [XIX.]—Practice of Cyprian and Ambrose.

What, then, hinders us, when we read of God's foreknowledge in some commentators on God's word, and they are treating of the calling of the elect, from understanding the same predestination? For they would perchance have rather used in this matter this word which, moreover, is better understood, and which is not inconsistent with, nay, is in accordance with, the truth which is declared concerning the predestination of grace. This I know, that no one has been able to dispute, except erroneously, against that predestination which I am maintaining in accordance with the Holy Scriptures. Yet I think that they who ask for the opinions of commentators on this matter ought to be satisfied with men so holy and so laudably celebrated everywhere in the faith and Christian doctrine as Cyprian and Ambrose, of whom I have given such clear testimonies; and that for both doctrines—that is, that they should both believe absolutely and preach everywhere that the grace of God is gratuitous, as we must believe and declare it to be; and that they should not think that preaching opposed to the preaching whereby we exhort the indolent or rebuke the evil; because these celebrated men also, although they were preaching God's grace in such a manner as that one of them said, "That we must boast in nothing, because nothing is our own;" and the other, "Our heart and our thoughts are not in our own power;" yet ceased not to exhort and rebuke, in order that the divine commands might be obeyed. Neither were they afraid of its being said to them, "Why do you exhort us, and why do you rebuke us, if no good thing that we have is from us, and if our hearts are not in our own power?" These holy men could by no means fear that such things should be said to them, since they were of the mind to understand that it is given to very few to receive the teaching of salvation through God Himself, or through the angels of heaven, without any human preaching to them; but that it is given to many to believe in God through human agency. Yet, in whatever manner the word of God is spoken to man, beyond a doubt for man to hear it in such a way as to obey it, is God's gift.

Chapter 49. —Further References to Cyprian and Ambrose.

Wherefore, the above-mentioned most excellent commentators on the divine declarations both preached the true grace of God as it ought to be preached, —that is, as a grace preceded by no human deservings, —and urgently exhorted to the doing of the divine commandments, that they who might have the gift of obedience should hear what commands they ought to obey. For if any merits of ours precede grace, certainly it is the merit of some deed, or word, or thought, wherein also is understood a good will itself. But he very briefly summed up the kinds of all deservings who said, "We must glory in nothing, because nothing is our own." And he who says, "Our heart and our thoughts are not in our own power," did not pass over acts and words also, for there is no act or word of man which does not proceed from the heart and the thought. But what more could that most glorious martyr and most luminous doctor Cyprian say concerning this matter, than when he impressed upon us that it behooves us to pray, in the Lord's Prayer, even for the adversaries of the Christian faith, showing what he thought of the beginning of the faith, that it also is God's gift, and pointing out that the Church of Christ prays daily for perseverance unto the end, because none but God gives that perseverance to those who have persevered? Moreover, the blessed Ambrose, when he was expounding the passage where the Evangelist Luke says, "It seemed good to me also," says, "What he declares to have seemed good to himself cannot have seemed good to him alone. For not alone by human will did it seem good, but as it pleased Him who speaks in me, Christ, who effects that that which is good may also seem good to us: for whom He has mercy on He also calls. And therefore he who follows Christ may answer, when he is asked why he wished to become a Christian, 'It seemed good to me also.' And when he says this, he does not deny that it seemed good to God; for the will of men is prepared by God. For it is God's grace that God should be honored by the saint." Moreover, in the same work, —that is, in the exposition of the same Gospel, when he had come to that place where the Samaritans would not receive the Lord when His face was as going to Jerusalem, —he says, "Learn at the same time that He would not be received by those who were not converted in simpleness of mind. For if He had been willing, He would have made them devout who were undevout. And why they would not receive Him, the evangelist himself mentioned, saying, 'Because

His face was as of one going towards Jerusalem.' But the disciples earnestly desired to be received into Samaria. But God calls those whom He makes worthy and makes religious whom He will." What more evident, what more manifest do we ask from commentators on God's word, if we are pleased to hear from them what is clear in the Scriptures? But to these two, who ought to be enough, let us add also a third, the holy Gregory, who testifies that it is the gift of God both to believe in God and to confess what we believe, saying, "I beg of you confess the Trinity of one godhead; but if ye wish otherwise, say that it is of one nature, and God will be besought that a voice shall be given to you by the Holy Spirit;" that is, God will be besought to allow a voice to be given to you by which you may confess what you believe. "For He will give, I am certain. He who gave what is first, will give also what is second." He who gave belief, will also give confession.

Chapter 50. —Obedience Not Discouraged by Preaching God's Gifts.

Such doctors, and so great as these, when they say that there is nothing of which we may boast as if of our own which God has not given us, and that our very heart and our thoughts are not in our own power; and when they give the whole to God, and confess that from Him we receive that we are converted to Him in such wise as to continue,—that that which is good appears also to us to be good, and we wish for it,—that we honor God and receive Christ,—that from undevout people we are made devout and religious,—that we believe in the Trinity itself, and also confess with our voice what we believe:— certainly attribute all these things to God's grace, acknowledge them as God's gifts, and testify that they come to us from Him, and are not from ourselves. But will anyone say that they in such wise confessed that grace of God as to venture to deny His foreknowledge, which not only learned but unlearned men also confess? Again, if they had so known that God gives these things that they were not ignorant that He foreknew that He would give them and could not have been ignorant to whom He would give them: beyond a doubt they had known the predestination which, as preached by the apostles, we laboriously and diligently maintain against the modern heretics. Nor would it be with any manner of justice said, nevertheless, to them because they preach obedience, and fervently exhort, to the extent of the ability of each one, to its practice, "If you do not wish that the obedience to which you are stirring us up should grow cold in our heart, forbear to preach to us that grace of God by which you confess that God gives what you are exhorting us to do."

Chapter 51 [XX.]—Predestination Must Be Preached.

Wherefore, if both the apostles and the teachers of the Church who succeeded them and imitated them did both these things,—that is, both truly preached the grace of God which is not given according to our merits, and inculcated by wholesome precepts a pious obedience,— what is it which these people of our time think themselves rightly bound by the invincible force of truth to say, "Even if what is said of the predestination of God's benefits be true, yet it must not be preached to the people"? It must absolutely be preached, so that he who has ears to hear, may hear. And who has them if he has not received them from Him who says, "I will give them a heart to know me, and ears to hear?" Assuredly, he who has not received may reject; while, yet, he who receives may take and drink, may drink and live. For as piety must be preached, that, by him who has ears to hear, God may be rightly worshipped; modesty must be preached, that, by him who has ears to hear, no illicit act may be perpetrated by his fleshly nature; charity must be preached, that, by him who has ears to hear, God and his neighbors may be loved;—so also must be preached such a predestination of God's benefits that he who has ears to hear may glory, not in himself, but in the Lord.

Chapter 52. —Previous Writings Anticipatively Refuted the Pelagian Heresy.

But in respect of their saying "that it was not necessary that the hearts of so many people of little intelligence should be disquieted by the uncertainty of this kind of disputation, since the catholic faith has been defended for so many years, with no less advantage, without this definition of predestination, as well against others as especially against the Pelagians, in so many books that have gone before, as well of Catholics and others as our own;" —I much wonder that they should say this, and not observe—to say nothing of other writings in this place—that those very treatises of mine were both composed and published before the Pelagians had begun to appear; and that they do not see in how many passages of those treatises I was unawares cutting down a future Pelagian heresy, by preaching the grace by which God delivers us from evil errors and from our habits, without any preceding merits of ours,—doing this according to His gratuitous mercy. And this I began more fully to apprehend in that disputation which I wrote to Simplicianus, the bishop of the Church of Milan, of blessed memory, in the beginning of my episcopate, when, moreover, I both perceived and asserted that the beginning of faith is God's gift.

Chapter 53. —Augustin's "Confessions."

And which of my smaller works has been able to be more generally and more agreeably known than the books of my Confessions? And although I published them before the Pelagian heresy had come into existence, certainly in them I said to my God, and said it frequently, "Give what Thou commands, and command what Thou wills." Which words of mine, Pelagius at Rome, when they were mentioned in his presence by a certain brother and fellow bishop of mine, could not bear; and contradicting somewhat too excitedly, nearly came to a quarrel with him who had mentioned them. But what, indeed, does God primarily and chiefly command, but that we believe on Him? And this, therefore, He Himself gives, if it is well said to Him, "Give what Thou commands." And, moreover, in those same books, in respect of what I have related concerning my conversion, when God converted me to that faith which, with a most miserable and raging talkativeness, I was destroying, do you not remember that it was so narrated how I showed that I was granted to the faithful and daily tears of my mother, that I should not perish? Where certainly I declared that God by His grace converted to the true faith the wills of men, which were not only averse to it, but even adverse to it. Further, in what manner I besought God concerning my growth in perseverance, you know, and you can review if you wish it. Therefore, that all the gifts of God which in that work I either asked for or praised, were foreknown by God that He would give, and that He could never be ignorant of the persons to whom He would give them, who can dare, I will not say to deny, but even to doubt? This is the manifest and assured predestination of the saints, which subsequently necessity compelled me more carefully and laboriously to defend when I was already disputing against the Pelagians. For I learnt that each special heresy introduced its own peculiar questions into the Church—against which the sacred Scripture might be more carefully defended than if no such necessity compelled their defense. And what compelled those passages of Scripture in which predestination is commended to be defended more abundantly and clearly by that labor of mine, than the fact that the Pelagians say that God's grace is given according to our merits; for what else is this than an absolute denial of grace?

Chapter 54 [XXI.]—Beginning and End of Faith is of God.

Therefore that this opinion, which is unpleasing to God, and hostile to those gratuitous benefits of God whereby we are delivered, may be destroyed, I maintain that both the beginning of faith and the perseverance therein, even to the end, are, according to the Scriptures—of which I have already quoted many—God's gifts. Because if we say that the beginning of faith is of ourselves, so that by it we deserve to receive other gifts of

God, the Pelagians conclude that God's grace is given according to our merits. And this the catholic faith held in such dread, that Pelagius himself, in fear of condemnation, condemned it. And, moreover, if we say that our perseverance is of ourselves, not of God, they answer that we have the beginning of our faith of ourselves in such wise as the end, thus arguing that we have that beginning of ourselves much more, if of ourselves we have the continuance unto the end, since to perfect is much greater than to begin; and thus repeatedly they conclude that the grace of God is given according to our merits. But if both are God's gifts, and God foreknew that He would give these His gifts (and who can deny this?), predestination must be preached, —that God's true grace, that is, the grace which is not given according to our merits, may be maintained with insuperable defense.

Chapter 55. —Testimony of His Previous Writings and Letters.

And, indeed, in that treatise of which the title is, Of Rebuke and Grace, which could not suffice for all my lovers, I think that I have so established that it is the gift of God also to persevere to the end, as I have either never before or almost never so expressly and evidently maintained this in writing, unless my memory deceives me. But I have now said this in a way in which no one before me has said it. Certainly the blessed Cyprian, in the Lord's Prayer, as I have already shown, so explained our petitions as to say that in its very first petition we were asking for perseverance, asserting that we pray for it when we say, "Hallowed be Thy name," although we have been already hallowed in baptism, —so that we may persevere in that which we have begun to be. Let those, however, to whom, in their love for me, I ought not to be ungrateful, who profess that they embrace, over and above that which comes into the argument, all my views, as you write,—let those, I say, see whether, in the latter portions of the first book of those two which I wrote in the beginning of my episcopate, before the appearance of the Pelagian heresy, to Simplicianus, the bishop of Milan, there remained anything whereby it might be called in question that God's grace is not given according to our merits; and whether I have not there sufficiently argued that even the beginning of faith is God's gift; and whether from what is there said it does not by consequence result, although it is not expressed, that even perseverance to the end is not given, except by Him who has predestinated us to His kingdom and glory. Then, did not I many years ago publish that letter which I had already written to the holy Paulinus, bishop of Nola, against the Pelagians, which they have lately begun to contradict? Let them also investigate that letter which I sent to Sixtus, the presbyter of the Roman Church when we contended in a very sharp conflict against the Pelagians, and they will find it such as is that one to Paulinus. Whence they may gather that the same sort of things were already said and written several years ago against the Pelagian heresy, and that it is to be wondered at that these should now displease them; although I should wish that no one would so embrace all my views as to follow me, except in those things in which he should see me not to have erred. For I am now writing treatises in which I have undertaken to retract my smaller works, for the purpose of demonstrating that even I myself have not in all things followed myself; but I think that, with God's mercy, I have written progressively, and not begun from perfection; since, indeed, I speak more arrogantly than truly, if even now I say that I have at length in this age of mine arrived at perfection, without any error in what I write. But the difference is in the extent and the subject of an error, and in the facility with which any one corrects it, or the pertinacity with which one endeavors to defend his error. Certainly, there is good hope of that man whom the last day of this life shall find so progressing that whatever was wanting to his progress may be added to him, and that he should be adjudged rather to need perfecting than punishment.

Chapter 56. —God Gives Means as Well as End.

Wherefore if I am unwilling to appear ungrateful to men who have loved me, because some advantage of my labor has attained to them before they loved me, how much rather am I unwilling to be ungrateful to God, whom we should not love unless He had first loved us and made us to love Him! since love is of Him, as they have said whom He made not only His great lovers, but also His great preachers. And what is more ungrateful than to deny the grace of God itself, by saying that it is given to us according to our merits? And this the catholic faith shuddered at in the Pelagians, and this it objected to Pelagius himself as a capital crime; and this Pelagius himself condemned, not indeed from love of God's truth, but yet for fear of his own condemnation. But whoever as a faithful catholic is horrified to say that the grace of God is given according to our merits, let him not withdraw faith itself from God's grace, whereby he obtained mercy that he should be faithful; and thus let him attribute also perseverance to the end to God's grace, whereby he obtains the mercy which he daily asks for, not to be led into temptation. But between the beginning of faith and the perfection of perseverance there are those means whereby we live righteously, which they themselves are agreed in regarding as given by God to us at the prayer of faith. And all these things—the beginning of faith, to wit, and His other gifts even to the end—God foreknew that He would bestow on His called. It is a matter therefore, of too excessive contentiousness to contradict predestination, or to doubt concerning predestination.

Chapter 57 [XXII.]—How Predestination Must Be Preached So as Not to Give Offence.

And yet this doctrine must not be preached to congregations in such a way as to seem to an unskilled multitude, or a people of slower understanding, to be in some measure confuted by that very preaching of it. Just as even the foreknowledge of God, which certainly men cannot deny, seems to be refuted if it be said to them, "Whether you run or sleep, you shall be that which He who cannot be deceived has foreknown you to be." And it is the part of a deceitful or an unskilled physician so to compound even a useful medicament, that it either does no good or does harm. But it must be said, "So run that you may lay hold; and thus by your very running you may know yourselves to be foreknown as those who should run lawfully:" and in whatever other manner the foreknowledge of God may be so preached, that the slothfulness of man may be repulsed.

Chapter 58. —The Doctrine to Be Applied with Discrimination.

Now, therefore, the definite determination of God's will concerning predestination is of such a kind that some from unbelief receive the will to obey and are converted to the faith or persevere in the faith, while others who abide in the delight of damnable sins, even if they have been predestinated, have not yet arisen, because the aid of pitying grace has not yet lifted them up. For if any are not yet called whom by His grace He has predestinated to be elected, they will receive that grace whereby they may will to be elected, and may be so; and if any obey, but have not been predestinated to His kingdom and glory, they are for a season, and will not abide in the same obedience to the end. Although, then, these things are true, yet they must not be so said to the multitude of hearers as that the address may be applied to themselves also, and those words of those people may be said to them which you have set down in your letter, and which I have above introduced: "The definite determination of God's will concerning predestination is of such a kind that some of you from unbelief shall receive the will to obey, and come to the faith." What need is there for saying, "Some of you"? For if we speak to God's Church, if we speak to believers, why do we say that "some of them" had come to the faith, and seem to do a wrong to the rest, when we may more fittingly say the definite determination of the will of God concerning predestination is of such a kind that from unbelief you shall receive the will to obey, and come to the faith, and shall receive perseverance, and abide to the end?

Chapter 59. —Offence to Be Avoided.

Neither is what follows by any means to be said,—that is, "But others of you who abide in the delight of sins have not yet arisen, because the aid of pitying grace has not yet lifted you up;" when it may be and ought to be well and conveniently said, "But if any of you are still delaying in the delightfulness of damnable sins, lay hold of the most wholesome discipline; and yet when you have done this be not lifted up, as if by your own works, nor boast as if you had not received this. For it is God who worketh in you both to will and to do for His good will, and your steps are directed by the Lord, so that you choose His way. But of your own good and righteous course, learn carefully that it is attributable to the predestination of divine grace."

Chapter 60. —The Application to the Church in General.

Moreover, what follows where it is said, "But yet if any of you are not yet called, whom by his grace He has predestinated to be called, you shall receive that grace whereby you shall will to be, and be, elected," is said more hardly than it could be said if we consider that we are speaking not to men in general, but to the Church of Christ. For why is it not rather said thus: "And if any of you are not yet called, let us pray for them that they may be called. For perchance they are so predestinated as to be granted to our prayers, and to receive that grace whereby they may will, and be made elected"? For God, who fulfilled all that He predestinated, has willed us also to pray for the enemies of the faith, that we might hence understand that He Himself also gives to the unbelievers the gift of faith, and makes willing men out of those that were unwilling.

Chapter 61. —Use of the Third Person Rather Than the Second.

But now I marvel if any weak brother among the Christian congregation can hear in any way with patience what relates to these words, when it is said to them, "And if any of you obey, if you are predestinated to be rejected, the power of obeying will be withdrawn from you, that you may cease to obey." For what does saying this seem, except to curse, or in a certain way to predict evils? But if, however, it is desirable or necessary to say anything concerning those who do not persevere, why is it not rather at least said in such a way as was a little while ago said by me,—first of all, so that this should be said, not of them who hear in the congregation, but about others to them; that is, that it should not be said, "If any of you obey, if you are predestinated to be rejected," but, "If any obey," and the rest, using the third person of the verb, not the second? For it is not to be said to be desirable, but abominable, and it is excessively harsh and hateful to fly as it were into the face of an audience with abuse, when he who speaks to them says, "And if there are any of you who obey, and are predestinated to be rejected, the power of obedience shall be withdrawn from you, that you may cease to obey." For what is wanting to the doctrine if it is thus expressed: "But if any obey, and are not predestinated to His kingdom and glory, they are only for a season, and shall not continue in that obedience unto the end"? Is not the same thing said both more truly and more fittingly, so that we may seem not as it were to be desiring so much for them, as to relate of others the evil which they hate, and think does not belong to them, by hoping and praying for better things? But in that way, they think that it must be said, the same judgment may be pronounced almost in the same words also of God's foreknowledge, which certainly they cannot deny, so as to say, "And if any of you obey, if you are foreknown to be rejected you shall cease to obey." Doubtless this is very true, assuredly it is; but it is very monstrous, very inconsiderate, and very unsuitable, not by its false declaration, but by its declaration not wholesomely applied to the health of human infirmity.

Chapter 62. —Prayer to Be Inculcated, Nevertheless.

But I do not think that manner which I have said should be adopted in the preaching of predestination ought to be sufficient for him who speaks to the congregation, except he adds this, or something of this kind, saying, "You, therefore, ought also to hope for that perseverance in obedience from the Father of Lights, from whom cometh down every excellent gift and every perfect gift, and to ask for it in your daily prayers; and in doing this ought to trust that you are not aliens from the predestination of His people, because it is He Himself who bestows even the power of doing this. And far be it from you to despair of yourselves, because you are bidden to have your hope in Him, not in yourselves. For cursed is everyone who has hope in man; and it is good rather to trust in the Lord than to trust in man, because blessed are all they that put their trust in Him. Holding this hope, serve the Lord in fear, and rejoice unto Him with trembling. Because no one can be certain of the life eternal which God who does not lie has promised to the children of promise before the times of eternity, —no one, unless that life of his, which is a state of trial upon the earth, is completed. But He will make us to persevere in Himself unto the end of that life, since we daily say to Him, 'Lead us not into temptation.'" When these things and things of this kind are said, whether to few Christians or to the multitude of the Church, why do we fear to preach the predestination of the saints and the true grace of God, —that is, the grace which is not given according to our merits, —as the Holy Scripture declares it? Or, indeed, must it be feared that a man should then despair of himself when his hope is shown to be placed in God, and should not rather despair of himself if he should, in his excess of pride and unhappiness, place it in himself?

Chapter 63 [XXIII.]—The Testimony of the Whole Church in Her Prayers.

And I wish that those who are slow and weak of heart, who cannot, or cannot as yet, understand the Scriptures or the explanations of them, would so hear or not hear our arguments in this question as to consider more carefully their prayers, which the Church has always used and will use, even from its beginnings until this age shall be completed. For of this matter, which I am now compelled not only to mention, but even to protect and defend against these new heretics, the Church has never been silent in its prayers, although in its discourses it has not thought that it need be put forth, as there was no adversary compelling it. For when was not prayer made in the Church for unbelievers and its opponents that they should believe? When has any believer had a friend, a neighbor, a wife, who did not believe, and has not asked on their behalf from the Lord for a mind obedient to the Christian faith? And who has there ever been who has not prayed for himself that he might abide in the Lord? And who has dared, not only with his voice, but even in thought, to blame the priest who invokes the Lord on behalf of believers, if at any time he has said, "Give to them, O Lord, perseverance in Thee to the end!" and has not rather responded, over such a benediction of his, as well with confessing lips as believing heart, "Amen"? Since in the Lord's Prayer itself the believers do not pray for anything else, especially when they say that petition, "Lead us not into temptation," save that they may persevere in holy obedience. As, therefore, the Church has both been born and grows and has grown in these prayers, so it has been born and grows and has grown in this faith, by which faith it is believed that God's grace is not given according to the merits of the receivers. For, certainly, the Church would not pray that faith should be given to unbelievers, unless it believed that God converts to Himself both the averse and adverse wills of men. Nor would the Church pray that it might persevere in the faith of Christ, not deceived nor overcome by the temptations of the world, unless it believed that the Lord has our heart in His power, in such wise as that the good which we do not hold save by our own will, we nevertheless do not hold except He worketh in us to will also. For if the Church indeed asks these things from Him, but thinks that the same things are given to itself by itself, it makes use of prayers which are not true, but perfunctory, —which be far from us! For who truly groans, desiring to receive what he prays for from the Lord, if he thinks that he receives it from himself, and not from the Lord?

Chapter 64. —In What Sense the Holy Spirit Solicits for Us, Crying, Abba, Father.

And this especially since "we know not what to pray for as we ought," says the apostle, "but the Spirit Himself makes intercession for us with groanings that cannot be uttered; and He that searches the hearts knows what is the mind of the Spirit, because He makes intercession for the saints according to God." What is "the Spirit Himself makes intercession," but, "causes to make intercession," "with groanings that cannot be uttered," but "truthful," since the Spirit is truth? For He it is of whom the apostle says in another place, "God hath sent the Spirit of His Son into our hearts, "crying, Abba, Father!" And here what is the meaning of "crying," but "making to cry," by that figure of speech whereby we call a day that makes people glad, a glad day? And this he makes plain elsewhere when he says, "For you have not received the Spirit of bondage again in fear, but you have received the Spirit of the adoption of sons, in whom we cry, Abba, Father." He there said, "crying," but here, "in whom we cry;" opening up, that is to say, the meaning with which he said "crying,"—that is, as I have already explained, "causing to cry," when we understand that this is also itself the gift of God, that with a true heart and spiritually we cry to God. Let them, therefore, observe how they are mistaken who think that our seeking, asking, knocking is of ourselves, and is not given to us; and say that this is the case because grace is preceded by our merits; that it follows them when we ask and receive, and seek and find, and it is opened to us when we knock. And they will not understand that this is also of the divine gift, that we pray; that is, that we ask, seek, and knock. For we have received the spirit of adoption of sons, in which we cry, Abba, Father. And this the blessed Ambrose also said. For he says, "To pray to God also is the work of spiritual grace, as it is written, No one says, Jesus is the Lord, but in the Holy Spirit."

Chapter 65. —The Church's Prayers Imply the Church's Faith.

These things, therefore, which the Church asks from the Lord, and always has asked from the time she began to exist, God so foreknew that He would give to His called, that He has already given them in predestination itself; as the apostle declares without any ambiguity. For, writing to Timothy, he says, "Labor along with the gospel according to the power of God, who saves us, and calls us with His holy calling, not according to our works, but according to His own purpose and grace, which was given us in Christ Jesus before the times of eternity, but is now made manifest by the coming of our Savior Jesus Christ." Let him, therefore, say that the Church at any time has not had in its belief the truth of this predestination and grace, which is now maintained with a more careful heed against the late heretics; let him say this who dares to say that at any time it has not prayed, or not truthfully prayed, as well that unbelievers might believe, as that believers might persevere. And if the Church has always prayed for these benefits, it has always believed them to be certainly God's gifts; nor was it ever right for it to deny that they were foreknown by

Him. And thus Christ's Church has never failed to hold the faith of this predestination, which is now being defended with new solicitude against these modern heretics.

Chapter 66 [XXIV.]—Recapitulation and Exhortation.

But what more shall I say? I think that I have taught sufficiently, or rather more than sufficiently, that both the beginning of faith in the Lord, and continuance in the Lord unto the end, are God's gifts. And other good things which pertain to a good life, whereby God is rightly worshipped, even they themselves on whose behalf I am writing this treatise concede to be God's gifts. Further, they cannot deny that God has foreknown all His gifts, and the people on whom He was going to bestow them. As, therefore, other things must be preached so that he who preaches them may be heard with obedience, so predestination must be preached so that he who hears these things with obedience may glory not in man, and therefore not in himself, but in the Lord; for this also is God's precept, and to hear this precept with obedience—to wit, that he who glories should glory in the Lord—in like manner as the rest, is God's gift. And he who has not this gift, —I shrink not from saying it, —whatever others he has, has them in vain. That the Pelagians may have this we pray, and that our own brethren may have it more abundantly. Let us not, therefore, be prompt in arguments and indolent in prayers. Let us pray, dearly beloved, let us pray that the God of grace may give even to our enemies, and especially to our brethren and lovers, to understand and confess that after that great and unspeakable ruin wherein we have all fallen in one, no one is delivered save by God's grace, and that grace is not repaid according to the merits of the receivers as if it were due, but is given freely as true grace, with no merits preceding.

Chapter 67. —The Most Eminent Instance of Predestination is Christ Jesus.

But there is no more illustrious instance of predestination than Jesus Himself, concerning which also I have already argued in the former treatise; and in the end of this I have chosen to insist upon it. There is no more eminent instance, I say, of predestination than the Mediator Himself. If any believer wishes thoroughly to understand this doctrine, let him consider Him, and in Him he will find himself also. The believer, I say; who in Him believes and confesses the true human nature that is our own, however singularly elevated by assumption by God the Word into the only Son of God, so that He who assumed, and what He assumed, should be one person in Trinity. For it was not a Quaternity that resulted from the assumption of man, but it remained a Trinity, since that assumption ineffably made the truth of one person in God and man. Because we say that Christ was not only God, as the Manichean heretics contend; nor only man, as the Photinian heretics assert; nor in such wise man as to have less of anything which of a certainty pertains to human nature,—whether a soul, or in the soul itself a rational mind, or flesh not taken of the woman, but made from the Word converted and changed into flesh,—all which three false and empty notions have made the three various and diverse parties of the Apollinarian heretics; but we say that Christ was true God, born of God the Father without any beginning of time; and that He was also true or very man, born of human mother in the certain fulness of time; and that His humanity, whereby He is less than the Father, does not diminish aught from His divinity, whereby He is equal to the Father. For both of them are One Christ—who, moreover, most truly said in respect of the God, "I and the Father are one;" and most truly said in respect of the man, "My Father is greater than I." He, therefore, who made of the seed of David this righteous man, who never should be unrighteous, without any merit of His preceding will, is the same who also makes righteous men of unrighteous, without any merit of their will preceding; that He might be the head, and they His members. He, therefore, who made that man with no precedent merits of His, neither to deduce from His origin nor to commit by His will any sin which should be remitted to Him, the same makes believers on Him with no preceding merits of theirs, to whom He forgives all sin. He who made Him such that He never had or should have an evil will, the same makes in His members a good will out of an evil one. Therefore He predestinated both Him and us, because both in Him that He might be our head, and in us that we should be His body, He foreknew that our merits would not precede, but that His doings should.

Chapter 68. —Conclusion.

Let those who read this, if they understand, give God thanks, and let those who do not understand, pray that they may have the inward Teacher, from whose presence comes knowledge and understanding. But let those who think that I am in error, consider again and again carefully what is here said, lest perchance they themselves may be mistaken. And when, by means of those who read my writings, I become not only wiser, but even more perfect, I acknowledge God's favor to me; and this I especially look for at the hands of the teachers of the Church, if what I write comes into their hands, and they condescend to acknowledge it.

www.ingramcontent.com/pod-product-compliance
Lightning Source LLC
Chambersburg PA
CBHW052110070526
44584CB00017B/2428